AMERICA HURRAH
AND OTHER PLAYS

AMERICA HURRAH
AND OTHER PLAYS

The Serpent
A Fable
The Hunter and The Bird
Almost Like Being

Jean-Claude van Itallie

Grove Press, Inc., New York

First Edition 1978
First Printing 1978
ISBN: 0-394-17039-3
Grove Press ISBN: 0-8021-4161-7
Library of Congress Catalog Card Number: 77-91355

Library of Congress Cataloging in Publication Data

  Van Itallie, Jean Claude, 1935-
    America hurrah and other plays.

     CONTENTS: America hurrah.—The serpent.—A fable.
—The hunter and the bird.—Almost like being.
     I. Title.
PS3572.A45A19   1978   812'.5'4   77-91355
ISBN 0-394-17039-3

Manufactured in the United States of America

Distributed by Random House, Inc., New York

GROVE PRESS, INC., 196 West Houston Street, New York, N.Y. 10014

AMERICA HURRAH

Introduction

by Robert Brustein

Just a few days ago, a director friend was trying to convince me that America stood on the brink of a theatrical renaissance that would produce at least ten dramatists of the first rank in the next few years. At the time I found this notion fairly preposterous but I am much more willing to entertain it now, having just returned from Jean-Claude van Itallie's three-play sequence, AMERICA HURRAH. I think I would respond to Mr. van Itallie's work under any circumstances— he speaks, if these plays are typical of him, more directly to my own particular obsessions than any other contemporary American playwright—but the important thing to note is that he does not function in isolation. The workshop and cabaret groups with which he has been associated have been collaborating with a surprising number of promising experimental dramatists, and one of these groups—the Open Theatre—has partly determined the development of his style.

The Open Theatre production of AMERICA HURRAH, in fact, is inseparable from the plays themselves, and the difficulty of the reviewer is in finding ways to praise the playwright without helping to deliver him over to the cultural cannibals. For if Mr. van Itallie provides the mind, spirit, and creative impulse of the evening, the Open Theatre actors provide the technique and invention, formed over three years of

Introduction to AMERICA HURRAH reprinted by permission of *The New Republic*, copyright © 1966 by Harrison-Blaine of New Jersey, Inc.

experimental work in histrionic transformation, and it would be criminal if the playwright's success led to any dissolution of this collaboration. With AMERICA HURRAH, the concept of theatrical unity finally becomes meaningful in this country and the American theatre takes three giant steps towards maturity.

The triumph of this occasion is to have found provocative theatrical images for the national malaise we have been suffering in Johnsonland these last three years: the infection of violence, calamity, indifference, gratuitous murder, and (probably the cause of all these) brutalizing war. In his first and most abstract short play, INTERVIEW, Mr. van Itallie examines, through a form of verbal and physical choreography, the mechanization of life in modern urban America. The setting is chalk white, broken by aluminum lines; four nervous job applicants from various classes of life are questioned by four bland interviewers in smiling shiny masks. The interview begins to reduce the applicants to a gaping, blinking chorus, and when they retreat into the air, the street completes the process. A young girl trying to find her way to Fourteenth Street runs a gauntlet of spastics, creeps, drunks, bizarre couples; a telephone operator is given cancer surgery with the actors transforming themselves into a failing respiratory machine; one unhappy man is given the usual ritual advice by his analyst ("Blah, blah, blah, blah, HOSTILE. Blah, blah, blah, blah, PENIS. Blah, blah, blah, blah, MOTHER. Blah, blah, blah, blah, MONEY.") while another is given customary silence by his priest; a candidate for governor dispenses hollow rhetoric on the subject of rats, red tape, four air, and Vietnam; and the play ends with the entire cast marching in place, their mouths opening and closing in a dehumanized language ("My fault" "Excuse me" "Can you help me?" "Next") from which all emotion has been evacuated. Joseph Chaikin, who founded the Open Theatre, has directed with keen imagination, finding the exact mechanical equivalents for the automatic movement of the play.

TV and MOTEL, both directed by the gifted Jacques Levy, are more particularized works, and both make their points through the interesting device of juxtaposition. TV, for example, which takes place in a television rating room, juxtaposes the eventless activities of three tired employees of the company with melodramatic scenes from familiar television programs (performed behind them by actors whose faces have been made up with video lines). The effect of this is to make a commonplace office reality act as a simple counterpoint to the grotesqueries taking place on the screen, thus obviating any need for satiric exaggeration (which mars most satire on the medium). While the office workers quarrel, joke, hold a birthday party, choke on chicken bones, etc., the television people enact the fantasies, crimes, and aberrations of contemporary America. Wonderboy, aided by his Wondervision, saves a housewife threatened by her monster husband; a news program tells of the accidental killing of 60 peasants in a friendly Vietnamese village, followed by a commercial for cigarettes; the Lily Heaven show brings us a loudmouthed pop singer with a Pepsodent smile, singing an endless finale to endless applause; a Billion Dollar movie about World War II ends with the reconciliation of two stiff lovers ("I've learned a lot. . . . Maybe that's what war is for."); Billy Graham addresses a crusade in Houston ("If we could look through the ceiling of this wonderful new air-conditioned stadium we could see the stars"), trying to reconcile great wealth with evangelical Christianity; a situation comedy, continually interrupted by canned laughter, revolves around the momentous question of why daughter isn't going to the prom. By the conclusion of the play, the three employees have become completely assimilated into the video action, though they haven't even been watching it, thus demonstrating, I assume, how mass culture has the power to break down our reality, whether we allow it to or not.

Mr. van Itallie's final short play is the most exciting of the evening, for it is based on a metaphor so powerful that it may well become the objective correlative of the Johnson age. Entitled MOTEL, it too is based on juxtapositions—of civilization and savagery, harmony and disorder, the nostalgic past and the terrifying present. Verbally, MOTEL is a monologue spoken by a female motelkeeper—the homey voice belongs to Ruth White, but the body is that of an enormous aproned doll with a huge carnival mask atop it, complete with hair rollers and glasses. The speech drones on about rooms ("rooms of marble and rooms of cork, all letting forth an avalanche"), rooms throughout history, and particularly this motel room with its antimacassars, hooked rugs, plastic flowers from Japan, television sets, toilets that automatically flush. As the motelkeeper proudly catalogues the room's possessions, the door opens with a blinding flash of headlights and a young couple enters—two more Artaudian mannikins on raised shoes, their huge heads bobbing, their bodies moving with the jerky menace of animated monsters. Gradually, they undress for the night, coming together for a grotesque papier mâché embrace, rubbing their cardboard bodies, then turn on the TV and, to the accompaniment of wild rock-and-roll, go about the cheerful destruction of the room: ripping off the toilet seat, breaking the bed springs, pulling down doors and windows, scrawling obscenities and pornographic drawings with lipstick on the walls, and finally tearing the motelkeeper apart, head and all. Vladimir Nabokov effectively used motel culture, in *Lolita*, as an image of the sordidness and tastelessness in the depths of our land; Mr. van Itallie uses it as an image of our violence, our insanity, our need to defile.

He has, in short, discovered the deepest poetic function of the theatre which is not, like most American dramatists, to absorb the audience into the author's own personal problems under the pretext that they are universal, but rather to invent metaphors which can poignantly suggest a nation's nightmares and afflictions. These metaphors solve nothing, change nothing, transform nothing, but they do manage to relax frustration and assuage loneliness by showing that it is still possible for men to share a common humanity—even if this only means sharing a common revulsion against what is mean and detestable. It is for this reason that I am exhilarated by these plays and by what they augur for the future of the American theatre.

AMERICA HURRAH, an evening of three short plays by Jean-Claude van Itallie, opened at the Pocket Theatre in New York City on November 7, 1966. Joseph Chaikin directed the first play, INTERVIEW. Jacques Levy directed TV and MOTEL. The producer was Stephanie Sills. Costumes: Tania Leontov. Stage Manager and Lighting Designer: Ken Glickfeld.

INTERVIEW

A Fugue for Eight Actors

INTERVIEW was first performed in 1965 (in an earlier version
and under the title PAVANE) at the Academy Theatre in At-
lanta. An Open Theatre production was directed at about the
same time by Peter Feldman; it was presented for one night
at the Sheridan Square Playhouse and then at the Cafe La
Mama. The La Mama Troupe performed the play in Europe
under the direction of Tom O'Horgan, who also directed the
play for National Educational TV. INTERVIEW would not exist
in its present form, however, without the collaboration, in
rehearsal, of Joseph Chaikin and the actors in AMERICA
HURRAH. The cast:

First Interviewer	Cynthia Harris
First Applicant	Conard Fowkes
Second Applicant	Ronnie Gilbert
Third Applicant	Henry Calvert
Fourth Applicant	Joyce Aaron
Second Interviewer	James Barbosa
Third Interviewer	Brenda Smiley
Fourth Interviewer	Bill Macy

The set is white and impersonal.

Two subway stairs are at the back of the stage. On the sides there is one entrance for Applicants and another entrance for Interviewers.

The only furniture or props needed are eight grey blocks.

The actors, four men and four women, are dressed in black-and-white street clothes. During the employment agency section only, Interviewers wear translucent plastic masks.

There is an intermittent harpsichord accompaniment: dance variations (minuet, Virginia reel, twist) on a familiar American tune. But much of the music (singing, whistling, humming) is provided by the actors on stage. It is suggested, moreover, that as a company of actors and a director approach the play they find their own variations in rhythmic expression. The successful transition from one setting to the next depends on the actors' ability to play together as a company and to drop character instantaneously and completely in order to assume another character, or for a group effect.

(*The First Interviewer for an employment agency, a young woman, sits on stage as the First Applicant, a Housepainter, enters.*)

FIRST INTERVIEWER (*standing*).   How do you do?

FIRST APPLICANT (*sitting*).   Thank you, I said, not knowing where to sit.

(*The characters will often include the audience in what they say, as if they were being interviewed by the audience.*)

FIRST INTERVIEWER (*pointedly*). Won't you sit down?

FIRST APPLICANT (*standing again quickly, afraid to displease*). I'm sorry.

FIRST INTERVIEWER (*busy with imaginary papers, pointing to a particular seat*). There. Name, please?

FIRST APPLICANT. Jack Smith.

FIRST INTERVIEWER. Jack what Smith?

FIRST APPLICANT. Beg pardon?

FIRST INTERVIEWER. Fill in the blank space, please. Jack blank space Smith.

FIRST APPLICANT. I don't have any.

FIRST INTERVIEWER. I asked you to sit down.
(*pointing*)
There.

FIRST APPLICANT (*sitting*). I'm sorry.

FIRST INTERVIEWER. Name, please?

FIRST APPLICANT. Jack Smith.

FIRST INTERVIEWER. You haven't told me your MIDDLE name.

FIRST APPLICANT. I haven't got one.

FIRST INTERVIEWER (*suspicious but writing it down*). No middle name.

(*Second Applicant, a woman, a Floorwasher, enters.*)

FIRST INTERVIEWER. How do you do?

SECOND APPLICANT (*sitting*). Thank you, I said, not knowing what.

FIRST INTERVIEWER. Won't you sit down?

SECOND APPLICANT (*standing*). I'm sorry.

FIRST APPLICANT. I am sitting.

FIRST INTERVIEWER (*pointing*). There. Name, please?

SECOND APPLICANT (*sitting*). Jane Smith.

FIRST APPLICANT. Jack Smith.

FIRST INTERVIEWER. What blank space Smith?

SECOND APPLICANT. Ellen.

FIRST APPLICANT. Haven't got one.

FIRST INTERVIEWER. What job are you applying for?

FIRST APPLICANT. Housepainter.

SECOND APPLICANT. Floorwasher.

FIRST INTERVIEWER. We haven't many vacancies in that. What experience have you had?

FIRST APPLICANT. A lot.

SECOND APPLICANT. Who needs experience for floorwashing?

FIRST INTERVIEWER. You will help me by making your answers clear.

FIRST APPLICANT. Eight years.

SECOND APPLICANT. Twenty years.

(*Third Applicant, a Banker, enters.*)

FIRST INTERVIEWER. How do you do?

SECOND APPLICANT. I'm good at it.

FIRST APPLICANT. Very well.

THIRD APPLICANT (*sitting*). Thank you, I said, as casually as I could.

FIRST INTERVIEWER. Won't you sit down?

THIRD APPLICANT (*standing again*). I'm sorry.

SECOND APPLICANT. I am sitting.

FIRST APPLICANT (*standing again*). I'm sorry.

FIRST INTERVIEWER (*pointing to a particular seat*). There. Name, please?

FIRST APPLICANT. Jack Smith.

SECOND APPLICANT. Jane Smith.

THIRD APPLICANT. Richard Smith.

FIRST INTERVIEWER. What EXACTLY Smith, please?

THIRD APPLICANT. Richard F.

SECOND APPLICANT. Jane Ellen.

FIRST APPLICANT. Jack None.

FIRST INTERVIEWER. What are you applying for?

FIRST APPLICANT. Housepainter.

SECOND APPLICANT. I need money.

THIRD APPLICANT. Bank president.

FIRST INTERVIEWER. How many years have you been in your present job?

THIRD APPLICANT. Three.

SECOND APPLICANT. Twenty.

FIRST APPLICANT. Eight.

(*Fourth Applicant, a Lady's Maid, enters.*)

FIRST INTERVIEWER. How do you do?

FOURTH APPLICANT. I said thank you, not knowing where to sit.

THIRD APPLICANT. I'm fine.

SECOND APPLICANT. Do I have to tell you?

FIRST APPLICANT. Very well.

FIRST INTERVIEWER. Won't you sit down?

FOURTH APPLICANT. I'm sorry.

THIRD APPLICANT (*sitting again*). Thank you.

SECOND APPLICANT (*standing again*). I'm sorry.

FIRST APPLICANT (*sitting*). Thanks.

FIRST INTERVIEWER (*pointing to a particular seat*). There. Name, please?

(*Fourth Applicant sits.*)

ALL APPLICANTS. Smith.

FIRST INTERVIEWER. What Smith?

FOURTH APPLICANT. Mary Victoria.

THIRD APPLICANT.   Richard F.

SECOND APPLICANT.   Jane Ellen.

FIRST APPLICANT.   Jack None.

FIRST INTERVIEWER.   How many years' experience have you had?

FOURTH APPLICANT.   Eight years.

SECOND APPLICANT.   Twenty years.

FIRST APPLICANT.   Eight years.

THIRD APPLICANT.   Three years four months and nine days not counting vacations and sick leave and the time both my daughters and my wife had the whooping cough.

FIRST INTERVIEWER.   Just answer the questions, please.

FOURTH APPLICANT.   Yes, sir.

THIRD APPLICANT.   Sure.

SECOND APPLICANT.   I'm sorry.

FIRST APPLICANT.   That's what I'm doing.

(*Second Interviewer, a young man, enters and goes to inspect Applicants. With the entrance of each Interviewer, the speed of the action accelerates.*)

SECOND INTERVIEWER. How do you do?

FIRST APPLICANT (*standing*). I'm sorry.

SECOND APPLICANT (*sitting*). Thank you.

THIRD APPLICANT (*standing*). I'm sorry.

FOURTH APPLICANT (*sitting*). Thank you.

SECOND INTERVIEWER. What's your name?

FIRST INTERVIEWER. Your middle name, please.

FIRST APPLICANT. Smith.

SECOND APPLICANT. Ellen.

THIRD APPLICANT. Smith, Richard F.

FOURTH APPLICANT. Mary Victoria Smith.

FIRST INTERVIEWER. What is your exact age?

SECOND INTERVIEWER. Have you any children?

FIRST APPLICANT. I'm thirty-two years old.

SECOND APPLICANT. One son.

THIRD APPLICANT. I have two daughters.

FOURTH APPLICANT. Do I have to tell you that?

FIRST INTERVIEWER.   Are you married, single, or other?

SECOND INTERVIEWER.   Have you ever earned more than that?

FIRST APPLICANT.   No.

SECOND APPLICANT.   Never.

THIRD APPLICANT.   Married.

FOURTH APPLICANT.   Single, NOW.

  (*Third Interviewer, a woman, enters.*)

THIRD INTERVIEWER.   How do you do?

FIRST APPLICANT (*sitting*).   Thank you.

SECOND APPLICANT (*standing*).   I'm sorry.

THIRD APPLICANT (*sitting*).   Thank you.

FOURTH APPLICANT (*standing*).   I'm sorry.

  (*Fourth Interviewer, a man, appears on the heels of Third Interviewer.*)

FOURTH INTERVIEWER.   How do you do?

FIRST APPLICANT (*standing*).   I'm sorry.

SECOND APPLICANT (*sitting*).   Thank you.

THIRD APPLICANT (*standing*).   I'm sorry.

FOURTH APPLICANT (*sitting*).   Thank you.

ALL INTERVIEWERS.   What is your Social Security Number, please?

(*Applicants do the next four speeches simultaneously.*)

FIRST APPLICANT.   333 dash 6598 dash 5590765439 dash 003.

SECOND APPLICANT.   999 dash 5733 dash 699075432 dash 11.

THIRD APPLICANT (*sitting*).   I'm sorry. I left it home. I can call if you let me use the phone.

FOURTH APPLICANT.   I always get it confused with my Checking Account Number.

(*Interviewers do the next four speeches in a round.*)

FIRST INTERVIEWER.   Will you be so kind as to tell me a little about yourself?

SECOND INTERVIEWER.   Can you fill me in on something about your background please?

THIRD INTERVIEWER.   It'd be a help to our employers if you'd give me a little for our files.

FOURTH INTERVIEWER.   Now what would you say, say, to a prospective employer about yourself?

(*Applicants address parts of the following four speeches, in particular, directly to the audience.*)

FIRST APPLICANT.   I've been a Union member twenty years, I said to them, if that's the kind of thing you want to know. Good health, I said. Veteran of two wars. Three kids. Wife's dead. Wife's sister, she takes care of them. I don't know why I'm telling you this, I said smiling.
(*sits*)

SECOND APPLICANT (*standing*).   So what do you want to know, I told the guy. I've been washin' floors for twenty years. Nobody's ever complained. I don't loiter after hours, I said to him. Just because my boy's been in trouble is no reason, I said, no reason—I go right home, I said to him. Right home.
(*sits*)

THIRD APPLICANT (*standing*).   I said that I was a Republican and we could start right there. And then I said that I spend most of my free time watching television or playing in the garden of my four-bedroom house with our two lovely daughters, aged nine and eleven. I mentioned that my wife plays with us too, and that her name is Katherine, although, I said casually, her good friends call her Kitty. I wasn't at all nervous.
(*sits*)

FOURTH APPLICANT (*standing*).   Just because I'm here, sir, I told him, is no reason for you to patronize me. I've been a lady's maid, I said, in houses you would not be allowed into. My father was a gentleman of leisure, AND what's more, I said, my references are unimpeachable.

FIRST INTERVIEWER. I see.

SECOND INTERVIEWER. All right.

THIRD INTERVIEWER. That's fine.

FOURTH INTERVIEWER. Of course.

(*Applicants do the following four speeches simultaneously.*)

FIRST APPLICANT. Just you call anybody at the Union and ask them. They'll hand me a clean bill of health.

SECOND APPLICANT. I haven't been to jail if that's what you mean. Not me. I'm clean.

THIRD APPLICANT. My record is impeccable. There's not a stain on it.

FOURTH APPLICANT. My references would permit me to be a governess, that's what.

FIRST INTERVIEWER (*going to First Applicant and inspecting under his arms*). When did you last have a job housepainting?

SECOND INTERVIEWER (*going to Second Applicant and inspecting her teeth*). Where was the last place you worked?

THIRD INTERVIEWER (*going to Third Applicant and inspecting him*). What was your last position in a bank?

FOURTH INTERVIEWER (*going to Fourth Applicant and inspecting her*). Have you got your references with you?

(*Applicants do the following four speeches simultaneously, with music under.*)

FIRST APPLICANT. I've already told you I worked right along till I quit.

SECOND APPLICANT. Howard Johnson's on Fifty-first Street all last month.

THIRD APPLICANT. First Greenfield International and Franklin Banking Corporation Banking and Stone Incorporated.

FOURTH APPLICANT. I've got a letter right here in my bag. Mrs. Muggintwat only let me go because she died.

(*Interviewers do the next four speeches in a round.*)

FIRST INTERVIEWER (*stepping around and speaking to Second Applicant*). Nothing terminated your job at Howard Johnson's? No franks, say, missing at the end of the day, I suppose?

SECOND INTERVIEWER (*stepping around and speaking to Third Applicant*). It goes without saying, I suppose, that you could stand an FBI Security Test?

THIRD INTERVIEWER (*stepping around and speaking to Fourth Applicant*). I suppose there are no records of minor thefts or, shall we say, borrowings from your late employer?

FOURTH INTERVIEWER (*stepping around and speaking to First Applicant*). Nothing political in your Union dealings? Nothing Leftist, I suppose? Nothing Rightist either, I hope.

(*Applicants and Interviewers line up for a square dance. Music under the following.*)

FIRST APPLICANT (*bowing to First Interviewer*). What's it to you, buddy?

SECOND APPLICANT (*bowing to Second Interviewer*). Eleanor Roosevelt wasn't more honest.

THIRD APPLICANT (*bowing to Third Interviewer*). My record is lily-white, sir!

FOURTH APPLICANT (*bowing to Fourth Interviewer*). Mrs. Thumbletwat used to take me to the bank and I'd watch her open her box!

(*Each Interviewer, during his next speech, goes upstage to form another line.*)

FIRST INTERVIEWER. Good!

SECOND INTERVIEWER. Fine!

THIRD INTERVIEWER. Swell!

FOURTH INTERVIEWER. Fine!

(*Applicants come downstage together; they do the next four speeches simultaneously and directly to the audience.*)

FIRST APPLICANT.   I know my rights. As a veteran. AND a citizen. I know my rights. AND my cousin is very well-known in certain circles, if you get what I mean. In the back room of a certain candy store in the Italian district of this city my cousin is VERY well known, if you get what I mean. I know my rights. And I know my cousin.

SECOND APPLICANT (*putting on a pious act, looking up to heaven*).   Holy Mary Mother of God, must I endure all the sinners of this earth? Must I go on a poor washerwoman in this City of Sin? Help me, oh my God, to leave this earthly crust, and damn your silly impudence, young man, if you think you can treat an old woman like this. You've got another thought coming, you have.

THIRD APPLICANT.   I have an excellent notion to report you to the Junior Chamber of Commerce of this city of which I am the Secretary and was in line to be elected Vice President and still will be if you are able to find me gainful and respectable employ!

FOURTH APPLICANT.   Miss Thumblebottom married into the Twiths and if you start insulting me, young man, you'll have to start in insulting the Twiths as well. A Twith isn't a nobody, you know, as good as a Thumbletwat, AND they all call me their loving Mary, you know.

ALL INTERVIEWERS (*in a loud raucous voice*).   Do you smoke?

(*Each Applicant, during his next speech, turns upstage.*)

FIRST APPLICANT.   No thanks.

SECOND APPLICANT. Not now.

THIRD APPLICANT. No thanks.

FOURTH APPLICANT. Not now.

ALL INTERVIEWERS (*again in a harsh voice and bowing or curtsying*). Do you mind if I do?

FIRST APPLICANT. I don't care.

SECOND APPLICANT. Who cares?

THIRD APPLICANT. Course not.

FOURTH APPLICANT. Go ahead.

(*Interviewers form a little group off to themselves.*)

FIRST INTERVIEWER. I tried to quit but couldn't manage.

SECOND INTERVIEWER. I'm a three-pack-a-day man, I guess.

THIRD INTERVIEWER. If I'm gonna go I'd rather go smoking.

FOURTH INTERVIEWER. I'm down to five a day.

(*Applicants all start to sneeze.*)

FIRST APPLICANT. Excuse me, I'm gonna sneeze.

SECOND APPLICANT. Have you got a hanky?

THIRD APPLICANT. I have a cold coming on.

FOURTH APPLICANT.   I thought I had some tissues in my bag.

(*Applicants all sneeze.*)

FIRST INTERVIEWER.   Gezundheit.

SECOND INTERVIEWER.   God bless you.

THIRD INTERVIEWER.   Gezundheit.

FOURTH INTERVIEWER.   God bless you.

(*Applicants all sneeze simultaneously.*)

FIRST INTERVIEWER.   God bless you.

SECOND INTERVIEWER.   Gezundheit.

THIRD INTERVIEWER.   God bless you.

FOURTH INTERVIEWER.   Gezundheit.

(*Applicants return to their seats.*)

FIRST APPLICANT.   Thanks, I said.

SECOND APPLICANT.   I said thanks.

THIRD APPLICANT.   Thank you, I said.

FOURTH APPLICANT.   I said thank you.

(*Interviewers stand on their seats and say the following as if one person were speaking.*)

FIRST INTERVIEWER. Do you

SECOND INTERVIEWER. speak any

THIRD INTERVIEWER. foreign

FOURTH INTERVIEWER. languages?

FIRST INTERVIEWER. Have you

SECOND INTERVIEWER. got a

THIRD INTERVIEWER. college

FOURTH INTERVIEWER. education?

FIRST INTERVIEWER. Do you

SECOND INTERVIEWER. take

THIRD INTERVIEWER. shorthand?

FOURTH INTERVIEWER. Have you

FIRST INTERVIEWER. any

SECOND INTERVIEWER. special

THIRD INTERVIEWER. qualifications?

FIRST INTERVIEWER. Yes?

FIRST APPLICANT (*stepping up to Interviewers*). Sure, I can speak Italian, I said. My whole family is Italian so I oughta be able to, and I can match colors, like green to green, so that even your own mother couldn't tell the difference, begging your pardon, I said, I went through the eighth grade.

(*steps back*)

SECOND INTERVIEWER.   Next.

SECOND APPLICANT (*stepping up to Interviewers*).   My grandmother taught me some Gaelic, I told the guy. And my old man could rattle off in Yiddish when he had a load on. I never went to school at all excepting church school, but I can write my name good and clear. Also, I said, I can smell an Irishman or a Yid a hundred miles off.

(*steps back*)

THIRD INTERVIEWER.   Next.

THIRD APPLICANT (*stepping up to Interviewers*).   I've never had any need to take shorthand in my position, I said to him. I've a Z.A. in business administration from Philadelphia, and a Z.Z.A. from M.Y.U. night school. I mentioned that I speak a little Spanish, of course, and that I'm a whiz at model frigates and warships.

(*steps back*)

FOURTH INTERVIEWER.   Next.

FOURTH APPLICANT (*stepping up to Interviewers*).   I can sew a straight seam, I said, hand or machine, and I have been exclusively a lady's maid although I CAN cook and will too if I have someone to assist me, I said. Unfortunately, aside from self-education, grammar school is as far as I have progressed.

(*steps back*)

(*Each Interviewer, during his next speech, bows or curtsies to the Applicant nearest him.*)

FIRST INTERVIEWER.   Good.

SECOND INTERVIEWER.   Fine.

THIRD INTERVIEWER.   Very helpful.

FOURTH INTERVIEWER.   Thank you.

(*Each Applicant, during his next speech, jumps on the back of the Interviewer nearest him.*)

FOURTH APPLICANT.   You're welcome, I'm sure.

THIRD APPLICANT.   Anything you want to know.

SECOND APPLICANT.   Just ask me.

FIRST APPLICANT.   Fire away, fire away.

(*The next eight speeches are spoken simultaneously, with Applicants on Interviewers' backs.*)

FIRST INTERVIEWER.   Well unless there's anything special you want to tell me, I think—

SECOND INTERVIEWER.   Is there anything more you think I should know about before you—

THIRD INTERVIEWER.   I wonder if we've left anything out of this questionnaire or if you—

FOURTH INTERVIEWER.   I suppose I've got all the information down here unless you can—

FIRST APPLICANT.   I've got kids to support, you know, and I need a job real quick—

SECOND APPLICANT.   Do you think you could try and get me something today because I—

THIRD APPLICANT.   How soon do you suppose I can expect to hear from your agency? Do you—

FOURTH APPLICANT.   I don't like to sound pressureful, but you know I'm currently on unemploy—

(*Each Applicant, during his next speech, jumps off Interviewer's back.*)

FIRST APPLICANT.   Beggin' your pardon.

SECOND APPLICANT.   So sorry.

THIRD APPLICANT.   Excuse me.

FOURTH APPLICANT.   Go ahead.

(*Each Interviewer, during his next speech, bows or curtsies and remains in that position.*)

FIRST INTERVIEWER.   That's quite all right.

SECOND INTERVIEWER.   I'm sorry.

THIRD INTERVIEWER.   I'm sorry.

FOURTH INTERVIEWER.   My fault.

(*Each Applicant, during his next speech, begins leap-frogging over Interviewers' backs.*)

FIRST APPLICANT.   My fault.

SECOND APPLICANT.   My fault.

THIRD APPLICANT.   I'm sorry.

FOURTH APPLICANT.   My fault.

(*Each Interviewer, during his next speech, begins leap-frogging too.*)

FIRST INTERVIEWER.   That's all right.

SECOND INTERVIEWER.   My fault.

THIRD INTERVIEWER.   I'm sorry.

FOURTH INTERVIEWER.   Excuse me.

(*The leap-frogging continues as the preceding eight lines are repeated simultaneously. Then the Interviewers confer in a huddle and come out of it.*)

FIRST INTERVIEWER.   Do you enjoy your work?

FIRST APPLICANT.   Sure, I said, I'm proud. Why not? Sure I know I'm no Rembrandt, I said, but I'm proud of my work, I said to him.

SECOND APPLICANT.   I told him it stinks. But what am I supposed to do, sit home and rot?

THIRD APPLICANT.   Do I like my work, he asked me. Well, I said, to gain time, do I like my work? Well, I said, I don't know.

FOURTH APPLICANT.   I told him right straight out: for a sensible person, a lady's maid is the ONLY POSSIBLE way of life.

SECOND INTERVIEWER.   Do you think you're irreplaceable?

ALL APPLICANTS.   Oh, yes indeed.

ALL INTERVIEWERS.   Irreplaceable?

ALL APPLICANTS.   Yes, yes indeed.

THIRD INTERVIEWER.   Do you like me?

FIRST APPLICANT.   You're a nice man.

SECOND APPLICANT.   Huh?

THIRD APPLICANT.   Why do you ask?

FOURTH APPLICANT.   It's not a question of LIKE.

FIRST INTERVIEWER.   Well, we'll be in touch with you.

(*This is the beginning of leaving the agency. Soft music under. Applicants and Interviewers push their seats into two masses of four boxes, one on each side of the stage. Applicants leave first, joining hands to form a revolving door.*

All are now leaving the agency, not in any orderly fashion. Interviewers start down one of the subway stairs at the back of the stage and Applicants start down the other. The following speeches overlap and are heard indistinctly as crowd noise.)

FOURTH INTERVIEWER.   What sort of day will it be?

FIRST APPLICANT.   I bet we'll have rain.

SECOND APPLICANT.   Cloudy, clearing in the afternoon.

THIRD APPLICANT.   Mild, I think, with some snow.

FOURTH APPLICANT.   Precisely the same as yesterday.

SECOND APPLICANT.   Can you get me one?

FIRST INTERVIEWER.   See you tomorrow.

THIRD APPLICANT.   When will I hear from you?

SECOND INTERVIEWER.   We'll let you know.

FOURTH APPLICANT.   Where's my umbrella?

THIRD INTERVIEWER.   I'm going to a movie.

FIRST APPLICANT.   So how about it?

FOURTH INTERVIEWER.   Good night.

THIRD APPLICANT.   Can you help me, Doctor, I asked.

(*When all of the actors are offstage, the Fourth Inter-viewer makes a siren sound and the following speeches continue from downstairs as a loud crowd noise for a few moments; they overlap so that the stage is empty only briefly.*)

FIRST INTERVIEWER.   It'll take a lot of work on your part.

SECOND INTERVIEWER.   I'll do what I can for you.

THIRD INTERVIEWER.   Of course I'll do my best.

FIRST INTERVIEWER.   God helps those who help themselves.

FIRST APPLICANT.   I have sinned deeply, Father, I said.

FIRST INTERVIEWER.   You certainly have. I hope you truly re-pent.

SECOND INTERVIEWER.   In the name of the Father, etcetera, and the Holy Ghost.

THIRD INTERVIEWER.   Jesus saves.

FOURTH APPLICANT.   I said can you direct me to Fourteenth Street, please?

FIRST INTERVIEWER.   Just walk down that way a bit and then turn left.

SECOND INTERVIEWER. Just walk down that way a bit and then turn right.

THIRD INTERVIEWER. Take a cab!

FOURTH APPLICANT. Do you hear a siren?

ALL INTERVIEWERS. What time is it?

FIRST APPLICANT. Half-past three.

SECOND APPLICANT. It must be about four.

THIRD APPLICANT. Half-past five.

FOURTH APPLICANT. My watch has stopped.

FIRST INTERVIEWER. Do you enjoy your work?

SECOND INTERVIEWER. Do you think you're irreplaceable?

THIRD INTERVIEWER. Do you like me?

(The actor who played the Fourth Interviewer comes on stage while continuing to make the loud siren noise. The actress who played the Fourth Applicant comes on stage and speaks directly to the audience.)

FOURTH APPLICANT. Can you direct me to Fourteenth Street, please, I said. I seem to have lost my—I started to say, and then I was nearly run down.

(The remaining actors return to the stage to play various people on Fourteenth Street: ladies shopping, a panhan-

*dler, a man in a sandwich board, a peddler of "franks
and orange," a snooty German couple, a lecher, a pair
of sighing lovers, and so on. The actors walk straight
forward toward the audience and then walk backwards
to the rear of the stage. Each time they approach the
audience, they do so as a different character. The actor
will need to find the essential vocal and physical manner-
isms of each character, play them, and drop them immediately to assume another character. The Fourth Applicant continues to address the audience directly, to in-
volve them in her hysteria, going up the aisle and back.)*

FOURTH APPLICANT. I haven't got my Social Security—I
started to say, I saw someone right in front of me and I
said, could you direct me please to Fourteenth Street, I have
to get to Fourteenth Street, please, to get a bargain, I explained, although I could hardly remember what it was I
wanted to buy. I read about it in the paper today, I said,
only they weren't listening and I said to myself, my pur-
pose for today is to get to—and I couldn't remember, I've
set myself the task of—I've got to have—it's that I can save,
I remembered, I can save if I can get that bargain at—and
I couldn't remember where it was so I started to look for
my wallet which I seem to have mislaid in my purse, and
a man—please watch where you're going, I shouted with
my purse half-open, and I seemed to forget—Fourteenth
Street, I remembered, and you'd think with all these num-
bered streets and avenues a person wouldn't get lost—you'd
think a person would HELP a person, you'd think so. So I
asked the most respectable looking man I could find, I
asked him, please can you direct me to Fourteenth Street.
He wouldn't answer. Just wouldn't. I'm lost, I said to myself. The paper said—the television said—they said, I

couldn't remember what they said. I turned for help: "Jesus Saves" the sign said, and a man was carrying it, both sides of his body, staring straight ahead. "Jesus Saves" the sign said.

(*The passers-by jostle her more and more.*)

FOURTH APPLICANT.   I couldn't remember where I was going. "Come and be saved" it said, so I asked the man with the sign, please, sir, won't you tell me how to, dear Lord, I thought, anywhere, please, sir, won't you tell me how to— can you direct me to Fourteenth Street, PLEASE!

(*The passers-by have covered the Fourth Applicant. All actors mill about until they reach designated positions on the stage where they face the audience, a line of women and a line of men, students in a gym class. The Second Interviewer has stayed coolly out of the crowd during this last; now he is the Gym Instructor.*)

GYM INSTRUCTOR.   I took my last puff and strode resolutely into the room. Ready men, I asked brightly. And one and two and three and four and one and two and keep it up.

(*The Gym Instructor is trying to help his students mold themselves into the kind of people seen in advertisements and the movies. As he counts to four the students puff out their chests, smile, and look perfectly charming. As he counts to four again, the students relax and look ordinary.*)

GYM INSTRUCTOR.   You wanna look like the guys in the movies, don't you, I said to the fellahs. Keep it up then. You

wanna radiate that kinda charm and confidence they have
in the movies, don't you, I said to the girls. Keep it up
then, stick 'em out, that's what you got 'em for. Don't be
ashamed. All of you, tuck in your butts, I said loudly.
That's the ticket, I said, wishing to hell I had a cigarette.
You're selling, selling all the time, that right, miss? Keep
on selling, I said. And one and two and three and four and
ever see that guy on TV, I said. What's his name, I asked
them. What's his name? Aw, you know his name, I said,
forgetting his name. Never mind, it'll come to you, I said.
He comes in here too. See that, I said, grabbing a guy out
of line and showing 'em his muscle. See that line, I said,
making the guy feel good, know what that is? It's boyish-
ness, I said. You come here, I said, throwing him back into
the line, and it'll renew your youthfulness, I said, taking a
deep breath. And one and two and three and four and
smile, I said, smiling. Not so big, I said, smiling less. You
look like creeps, I said, when you smile that big. When you
smile, hold something back. Make like you're holding back
something big, I said, a secret, I said. That's the ticket.
And one and two and three and four and . . .
   (*accelerating the rhythm to a double count*)
Anybody got a cigarette, I said suddenly, without thinking.
I was just kidding, I said then, sheepishly. One and two
and three and four, I said, wishing I had a cigarette. And
one and two and three and four . . .

   (*The rapid movements of the gym class become the vi-
brations of passengers on a moving subway train. The
actors rush to the boxes stage left, continuing to vibrate.
Two of the actors stand on the boxes and smile like subway advertisements while the others, directly in front of
them, are pushed against each other on the crowded*

*train. They make an appropriate soft subway noise, a
kind of rhythmic hiss and, as the subway passengers, form
their faces into frozen masks of indifference.)*

SECOND APPLICANT (*squeezing her way to an uncomfortable
front seat and speaking half to herself*).   God forgive me
. . . you no-good chump, I said to him, I used to love
you . . . not now. Not now . . . God forgive me . . .
God forgive me for being old. Not now, I said. I wouldn't
wipe the smell off your uncle's bottom now, not for turnips,
no. God forgive me . . . Remember how we used to ride
the roller coaster out at Coney Island, you and me? Remember? Holding hands in the cold and I'd get so scared
and you'd get so scared and we'd hug each other and buy
another ticket . . . Remember? . . . Look now, I said.
Look at me now! God forgive you for leaving me with
nothing . . . God forgive you for being dead . . . God
forgive me for being alive . . .

(*The actress who played the Third Interviewer slips out
of the subway as though it were her stop and sits on a
box, stage right, as a Telephone Operator. The other
actors form a telephone circuit by holding hands in two
concentric circles around the boxes, stage left; they
change the hissing sound of the subway into the whistling
of telephone circuits.*)

TELEPHONE OPERATOR.   Just one moment and I will connect
you with Information.

(*The Telephone Operator alternates her official voice
with her ordinary voice; she uses the latter when she
talks to her friend Roberta, another operator whom she*

reaches by flipping a switch. When she is talking to Roberta, the whistling of the telephone circuit changes into a different rhythm and the arms of the actors, which are forming the circuit, move into a different position.)

TELEPHONE OPERATOR.   Just one moment and I will connect you with Information. Ow! Listen, Roberta, I said, I've got this terrible cramp. Hang up and dial again, please; we find nothing wrong with that number at all. You know what I ate, I said to her, you were there. Baked macaroni, Wednesday special, maple-nut fudge, I said. I'm sorry but the number you have reached is not—I can feel it gnawing at me at the bottom of my belly, I told her. Do you think it's serious, Roberta? Appendicitis? I asked. Thank you for giving us the area code but the number you have reached is not in this area. Roberta, I asked her, do you think I have cancer? One moment, please, I'm sorry the number you have reached—ow! Well, if it's lunch, Roberta, I said to her, you know what they can do with it tomorrow. Ow! One moment, please, I said. Ow, I said, Roberta, I said, it really hurts.

(The Telephone Operator falls off her seat in pain. The whistling of the telephone circuit becomes a siren. Three actors carry the Telephone Operator over to the boxes, stage left, which now serve as an operating table. Three actors imitate the Telephone Operator's breathing pattern while four actors behind her make stylized sounds and movements as surgeons and nurses in the midst of an operation. The Telephone Operator's breathing accelerates, then stops. After a moment the actors begin spreading over the stage and making the muted sounds of a cocktail party: music, laughter, talk. The actors find

*a position and remain there, playing various aspects of a
party in slow motion and muted tones. They completely
ignore the First Interviewer who, as a Girl At The Party,
goes from person to person as if she were in a garden of
living statues.*)

GIRL AT THE PARTY (*rapidly and excitedly*).   And then after
the ambulance took off I went up in the elevator and into
the party. Did you see the accident, I asked, and they said
they did, and what did he look like, and I said he wore a
brown coat and had straight brown hair. He stepped off
the curb right in front of me. We had been walking up
the same block, he a few feet ahead of me, this block right
here, I said, but she wasn't listening. Hi, my name is Jill,
I said to somebody sitting down and they looked at me and
smiled so I said his arm was torn out of its socket and his
face was on the pavement gasping but I didn't touch him
and she smiled and walked away and I said after her, you
aren't supposed to touch someone before—I WANTED to
help, I said, but she wasn't listening. When a man came
up and said was it someone you knew and I said yes, it
was someone I knew slightly, someone I knew, yes, and
he offered me a drink and I said no thanks, I didn't want
one, and he said well how well did I know him, and I said
I knew him well, yes, I knew him very well. You were
coming together to the party, he said. Yes, I said, excuse
me. Hi, my name is Jill, did you hear a siren, and they said
oh you're the one who saw it, was he killed?

(*becoming resigned to the fact that no one is listening*)
And I said yes I was, excuse me, and went back across the
room but couldn't find another face to talk to until I deliberately bumped into somebody because I had to tell
them one of us couldn't come because of the accident. It

was Jill. Jill couldn't come. I'm awfully sorry, I said, because of the accident. She had straight brown hair, I said, and was wearing a brown coat, and two or three people looked at me strangely and moved off. I'm sorry, I said to a man, and I laughed, and moved off. I'm dead, I said to several people and started to push them over, I'm dead, thank you, I said, thank you, please, I said, I'm dead, until two or three of them got hold of my arms and hustled me out. I'm sorry, I said, I couldn't come because of the accident. I'm sorry. Excuse me.

(*The Girl At The Party is lowered to the floor by two of the men and then all fall down except the actor who played the Fourth Interviewer. He remains seated as a Psychiatrist. The Third Applicant, on the floor, props his head up on his elbow and speaks to the audience.*)

THIRD APPLICANT. Can you help me, Doctor, I asked him.

(*The Psychiatrist crosses his legs and assumes a professional expression.*)

THIRD APPLICANT. Well, it started, well it started, I said, when I was sitting in front of the television set with my feet on the coffee table. Now I've sat there hundreds of times, thousands maybe, with a can of beer in my hand. I like to have a can of beer in my hand when I watch the beer ads. But now for no reason I can think of, the ad was making me sick. So I used the remote control to get to another channel, but each channel made me just as sick. The television was one thing and I was a person, and I was going to be sick. So I turned it off and had a panicky moment. I smelled the beer in my hand and as I vomited I looked around the living room for something to grab on to, something to look at, but there was just our new furniture. I tried to get a hold of myself. I tried to stare straight ahead above the television set, at a little spot on the wall I know. I've had little moments like that before, Doctor, I said, panicky little moments like that when the earth seems to slip out from under, and everything whirls around and you try to hold onto something, some object, some thought, but I couldn't think of anything. Later the panic went away, I told him, it went away, and I'm much better now. But I don't feel like doing anything anymore, except sit and stare at the wall. I've lost my job. Katherine thought I should come and see you. Can you help me, Doctor, I asked him.

PSYCHIATRIST
 Blah, blah, blah, blah, blah, blah, HOSTILE.
 Blah, blah, blah, blah, blah, blah, PENIS.
 Blah, blah, blah, blah, blah, blah, MOTHER.
 (*holding out his hand*)
 Blah, blah, blah, blah, blah, blah, MONEY.

(*The Third Applicant takes the Psychiatrist's hand and gets up, extending his left hand to the next actor. This begins a grand right and left with all the actors all over the stage.*)

ALL (*chanting as they do the grand right and left*).
 Blah, blah, blah, blah, blah, blah, HOSTILE.
 Blah, blah, blah, blah, blah, blah, PENIS.
 Blah, blah, blah, blah, blah, blah, MOTHER.
 Blah, blah, blah, blah, blah, blah, MONEY.
 Blah, blah, blah, blah, blah, blah, HOSTILE.

Blah, blah, blah, blah, blah, blah, PENIS.
Blah, blah, blah, blah, blah, blah, MOTHER.
Blah, blah, blah, blah, blah, blah, MONEY.
(*forming couples and locking hands with arms crossed, continuing to move, but in a smaller circle*)
Blah, blah, blah, blah, blah, blah, blah.
Blah, blah, blah, blah, blah, blah, blah.

(*Now they slow down to the speed of a church procession. The women bow their heads, letting their hair fall forward over their faces. The "blah, blah, blah" continues, but much more slowly while some of the women accompany it with a descant of "Kyrie Eleison." After they have gone around in a circle once this way, the actor who played the Fourth Interviewer sits with his back to the audience as a Priest. The First Applicant kneels next to him, facing the audience as if in a confessional booth. The other six actors are at the back of the stage in two lines, swaying slightly, heads down. The women are in front with their hair still down over their faces.*)

FIRST APPLICANT (*crossing himself perfunctorily and starting to speak; his manner is not impassioned; it is clear that he comes regularly to repeat this always fruitless ritual*).   Can you help me, Father, I said, as I usually do, and he said, as usual, nothing. I'm your friend, the housepainter, I said, the good housepainter. Remember me, Father? He continued, as usual, to say nothing. Almost the only color you get to paint these days, Father, I said, is white. Only white, Father, I said, not expecting any more from him than usual, but going on anyway. The color I really like to paint, Father, is red, I said. Pure brick red. Now there's a confession, Father. He said nothing. I'd like to take a trip to the country, Father, I said, and paint a barn door red, thinking that would get a rise out of him, but it didn't. God, I said then, deliberately taking the Lord's name in vain, the result of taking a three-inch brush and lightly kissing a coat of red paint on a barn door is something stunning and beautiful to behold. He still said nothing. Father, I said, springing it on him, Father, I'd like to join a monastery. My wife's sister, she could take care of the kids. Still nothing. Father, I said again, I'd like to join a monastery. Can you help me, Father? Nothing. Father, I said, I've tried lots of things in my life, I've gone in a lot of different directions, Father, and none of them seems any better than any other, Father, I said. Can you help me, Father, I said. But he said nothing as usual, and then, as usual, I went away.

(*The First Applicant and the Fourth Interviewer, who haven't moved at all during the confession, move upstage to join the others as the music starts up violently in a rock beat. The actors do a rock version of the Virginia reel.*)

SECOND INTERVIEWER (*loudly*). My

(*All bow to partners.*)

FOURTH APPLICANT (*loudly*). fault.

(*All dos-à-dos.*)

SECOND APPLICANT (*loudly*). Excuse

(*All circle around.*)

FOURTH INTERVIEWER (*loudly*).   me.

(*All peel off.*)

FIRST INTERVIEWER (*loudly*).   Can you

SECOND APPLICANT (*loudly*).   help

FIRST APPLICANT (*loudly*).   me?

FOURTH INTERVIEWER (*loudly*).   Next.

(*All continue dancing, joining hands at the center to form a revolving door again. They repeat the preceding eight speeches. Then the Second Interviewer speaks rapidly, as a Square Dance Caller.*)

SQUARE DANCE CALLER.   Step right up, ladies and gents, and shake the hand of the next governor of this state. Shake his hand and say hello. Tell your friends you shook the hand of the next governor of the state. Step right up and shake his hand. Ask him questions. Tell him problems. Say hello. Step right up, shake his hand, shake the hand, ladies and gents, of the next governor of the state. Tell your folks: I shook his hand. When he's famous you'll be proud. Step right up, ladies and gents, and shake his hand. Ask him questions. Tell him problems. Say hello. Step right up, ladies and gents. Don't be shy. Shake the hand of the next governor of this state.

(*The actors have formed a crowd, downstage right, facing the audience. They give the impression of being but a few of a great number of people, all trying to squeeze*

*to the front to see and speak to the political candidate.
The Fourth Interviewer, now playing a Politician, stands
on a box, stage left, facing the audience. The Second
Interviewer stands by the crowd and keeps it in order.)*

POLITICIAN. Thank you very much, I said cheerfully, and
good luck to you, I said, turning my smile to the next one.

*(The First Interviewer, panting as the Girl At The Party,
squeezes out of the crowd and rushes up to the Politician,
who smiles at her benignly.)*

POLITICIAN. Our children ARE our most important asset, I
agreed earnestly. Yes they are, I said solemnly. Children,
I said, with a long pause, are our most important asset. I
only wish I could, madame, I said earnestly, standing tall,
but rats, I said regretfully, are a city matter.

*(The First Interviewer returns to the crowd while the
Third Interviewer, as the Telephone Operator, rushes up
to the Politician. She appeals to him, making the same
noise she made when her stomach hurt her.)*

POLITICIAN. Nobody knows more about red tape than I do,
I said knowingly, and I wish you luck, I said, turning my
smile to the next one.

*(The Third Interviewer returns to the crowd and the
Fourth Applicant goes up to the Politician.)*

POLITICIAN. I certainly will, I said, with my eyes sparkling,
taking a pencil out of my pocket. And what's your name,

I said, looking at her sweetly and signing my name at the same time. That's a lovely name, I said.

(*The Fourth Applicant returns to the crowd while the Third Applicant, as an Older Man, shakes the Politician's hand.*)

POLITICIAN. Yes sir, I said, those were the days. And good luck to you, sir, I said respectfully but heartily, and look out for the curb, I said, turning my smile to the next one.

(*The Third Applicant returns to the crowd and the Second Applicant approaches the Politician.*)

POLITICIAN. Indeed yes, the air we breathe is foul, I said indignantly. I agree with you entirely, I said wholeheartedly. And if my opponent wins it's going to get worse, I said with conviction. We'd all die within ten years, I said. And good luck to you, madame, I said politely, and turned my smile to the next one.

(*The First Applicant approaches him, his cap in his hand.*)

POLITICIAN. Well, I said confidingly, getting a bill through the legislature is easier said than done, and answering violence, I said warningly, with violence, I said earnestly, is not the answer, and how do you do, I said, turning my smile to the next one.

(*Next, two Sighing Lovers—we saw them on Fourteenth Street—played by the First and Second Interviewers, approach the Politician.*)

POLITICIAN. No, I said, I never said my opponent would kill us all. No, I said, I never said that. May the best man win, I said manfully.

(*Half-hearted cheers. The First and Second Interviewers return to the crowd.*) ·

POLITICIAN. I do feel, I said without false modesty, that I'm better qualified in the field of foreign affairs than my opponents are, yes, I said, BUT, I said, with a pause for emphasis, foreign policy is the business of the President, not the Governor, therefore I will say nothing about the war, I said with finality.

(*The crowd makes a restive sound, then freezes.*)

POLITICIAN. Do you want us shaking hands, I asked the photographer, turning my profile to the left. Goodbye, I said cheerfully, and good luck to you too.

(*The crowd makes a louder protest, then freezes.*)

POLITICIAN. I'm sorry, I said seriously, but I'll have to study that question a good deal more before I can answer it.

(*The crowd makes an angry noise, then freezes.*)

POLITICIAN. Of course, I said frowning, we must all support the President, I said as I turned concernedly to the next one.

(*The crowd makes a very angry sound, then freezes.*)

POLITICIAN.   I'm sorry about the war, I said. Nobody could
be sorrier than I am, I said sorrowfully. But I'm afraid, I
said gravely, that there are no easy answers.
  (*smiles, pleased with himself*)
Good luck to you too, I said cheerfully, and turned my
smile to the next one.   ·

  (*The Politician topples from his box, beginning his
  speech all over again. Simultaneously, all the other actors
  lurch about the stage, speaking again in character: the
  Shopper On Fourteenth Street, the Gym Instructor, the
  Subway Rider, the Telephone Operator, the Girl At The
  Party, the Analysand, and the Housepainter. Simultaneously, they all stop and freeze, continue again, freeze
  again, then continue with music under. The Second Interviewer, acting as policeman, begins to line them up
  in a diagonal line, like marching dolls, one behind the
  other. As they are put into line they begin to move their
  mouths without sound, like fish in a tank. The music
  stops. When all are in line the Second Interviewer joins
  them.*)

SECOND INTERVIEWER.   My

FOURTH APPLICANT.   fault.

SECOND APPLICANT.   Excuse

FOURTH INTERVIEWER.   me.

FIRST INTERVIEWER.   Can you

SECOND APPLICANT.   help

FIRST APPLICANT.   me?

FOURTH INTERVIEWER.   Next.

(*All continue marching in place, moving their mouths, and shouting their lines as the lights come slowly down.*)

SECOND INTERVIEWER.   My

FOURTH APPLICANT.   fault.

SECOND APPLICANT.   Excuse

FOURTH INTERVIEWER.   me.

FIRST INTERVIEWER.   Can you

SECOND APPLICANT.   help

FIRST APPLICANT.   me?

FOURTH INTERVIEWER.   Next.

TV

The youth Narcissus mistook his own reflection in the water
for another person ... He was numb. He had adapted to his
extension of himself and had become a closed system.

Marshall McLuhan

TV was premiered as part of the AMERICA HURRAH production at the Pocket Theatre in New York City.

The cast:

Conard Fowkes as Hal

Brenda Smiley   as Susan

Bill Macy   as George

Ronnie Gilbert as Helen Fargis, the President's wife, a UGP researcher, a member of the rock and roll group, a peace marcher, Lily Heaven, the headache sufferer, a singer in the evangelist choir, and Mother in "My Favorite Teenager"

Henry Calvert   as Harry Fargis, First News Announcer, Steve, the President, a UGP researcher, a member of the rock and roll group, Weather Announcer, He in the Billion Dollar Movie, Evangelist, and Father in "My Favorite Teenager"

James Barbosa   as   Wonderboy, Second News Announcer, the man in the cigarette commercial, Bill, UGP Announcer, a member of the rock and roll group, one young man from New York City, Lily Heaven's Announcer, Ron Campbell, Johnny Holland, and a singer in the evangelist choir

Cynthia Harris   as   the woman in the cigarette commercial, the President's older daughter, a UGP researcher, a member of the rock and roll group, a peace marcher, Famous Television Personality, Carol, She in the Billion Dollar Movie, and a singer in the evangelist choir

Joyce Aaron   as   Sally, the President's younger daughter, the Spanish teacher, a UGP researcher, a member of the rock and roll group, Annie Kappelhoff, Lady Announcer, Luci, a singer in the evangelist choir, and Daughter in "My Favorite Teenager"

Slides: drawings by Francisca Duran-Reynals
        photographs by Phill Niblock and Martin Bough

Make-up: Remy Charlip

Design for printed script: Sharon Thie

The set is white and impersonal. There are two doors on the stage right wall: one leads to the rest rooms, the other to the hall.

Downstage right is the control console in a television viewing room. It faces the audience.

Above the console, also facing the audience, is a screen. Projected on it, from the rear, is the logo of a television station.

Downstage left is a water cooler, a closet for coats, and a telephone. Downstage right is a bulletin board. Upstage center is a table with a coffee maker on it.

Hal and Susan are seated at the console, Susan in the middle chair. They are both in their twenties. Hal is playing, as he often will, with his penknife: whittling pencils, paring his nails, or throwing it at the bulletin board. Susan is involved with the papers on the console, with sharpening pencils, and so forth.

At the back of the stage, on the left, are the five actors who will portray what will appear on television. For the moment they have no light on them and their backs are to the audience.

To indicate the correlation of the events and dialogue on television with those which occur in the viewing room, the play is printed in two columns.

HAL

So what do you say?

SUSAN

I don't know.

HAL

That doesn't get us very far, does it?

SUSAN

Well it's such a surprise,
your asking. I was plan-
ning to work on my apart-
ment.

HAL

I'll help you, after the
movie.

SUSAN

That's too late. One thing
I have to have is eight
hours' sleep. I really have
to have that.

(*George enters; he is
older than Hal and Su-
san, and is in charge of
the viewing room.*)

HAL

Hi, George.

SUSAN

Hello, George.

GEORGE (*to Susan*)
Is that a new dress?

SUSAN (*nodding toward Hal*)
HE didn't even notice.

> (*George puts his coat
> and jacket in the closet
> and puts on a cardigan
> sweater.*)

GEORGE
How many check marks
have you made, Hal?

HAL
I don't know, George. I
don't count.

SUSAN
I got it on Fourteenth
Street. I love going into
places like that because
they're so cheap.

GEORGE
If you don't make at least
a hundred check marks,
they'll dock you. That's
what the totals count col-
umn is for.

SUSAN (*looking at herself in
a mirror*)
Have I lost any weight?

GEORGE
Where would you lose it
from?

HAL

George, how come they
haven't asked us for a de-
tailed report in nearly
three weeks?

GEORGE

How should I know?

HAL

Think they're forgetting
about us, George?

SUSAN

I was trying to tell in the
Ladies, but the fluorescent
light in there just burns
your eyes.

HAL

I've never been to the
Ladies. You think I'd like
it?

GEORGE

This viewing room is the
backbone of the rating system.

HAL

He said that to you LAST
month, George. Things
move fast.

GEORGE
Are you trying to make
me nervous?

HAL
Maybe.

GEORGE
Well don't, because my
stomach is not very good
this morning.

SUSAN
I want to know seriously,
and I mean seriously, do
you think I've lost any
weight?

GEORGE
Where from?

HAL
Why don't you let your-
self go?

SUSAN
What do you mean?

HAL
Just let nature take its
course.

SUSAN

What if nature wants you
to be a big fat slob?

HAL

Then be a big fat slob.

SUSAN

Thanks.

(*Hal, Susan, and George sit down and get ready for the
day's work. George turns a dial on the console which
turns on TV. Two of the People On Television turn
around to play Helen and Harry Fargis.*

*All of the People On Television are dressed in shades of
gray. They make no costume changes and use no real
props. Their faces are made up with thin horizontal black
lines to suggest the way they might appear to a viewer.
They are playing television images. Their style of acting
is cool, not pushy. As television characters, they have only
a few facial masks, such as "cute," "charming," or "serious," which they use infallibly, like signals, in the course
of each television segment.*

*After each television segment, the People involved in it
will freeze where they are until it is time for them to
become another character.*

*As the play progresses, the People On Television will use
more and more of the stage. The impression should be
that of a slow invasion of the viewing room. Hal, Susan,
and George will simply move around the People On Tele-*

vision when that becomes necessary. Ultimately, the control console itself will be taken over by television characters, so that the distinction between what is on television and what is occurring in the viewing room will be lost completely.

The attention of the audience should be focused not on a parody of television, but on the relationship of the life that appears on television to the life that goes on in the viewing room.

All of the actors will need to be constantly aware of what is happening on all parts of the stage, in order to give and take the attention of the audience to and from each other, and also in order to demonstrate the influence of the style of certain television segments on the behavior of Hal, Susan, and George.)

(Slide on screen: Wonderboy's face.)

HAL
Why try to look like somebody else?

(Helen and Harry Fargis are at home. Helen is baking cookies.)

HELEN
Harry, what are you working on in the garage?

SUSAN
I'm trying to look like myself, thin. Very thin.

HARRY
If I succeed in my experiments, nobody in the world will be hungry for love. Ever again.

HAL (*offering him one*)
Want a cigarette, George?

GEORGE
No, thanks.

HELEN
Hungry for love? Harry, you make me nervous.

HAL
Just one?

HELEN
You really do.

GEORGE
No.

HARRY
Men will put down their arms.

SUSAN
Hal, why don't you try to help George instead of being so cruel?

HELEN
You haven't been to work for a week now. You'll lose your job.

HAL
I'm just offering him a cigarette.

HARRY
You don't understand.
This is more important.

HELEN
Oh, Harry. I don't under-
stand you at all any more.
I really don't.

GEORGE (*as Hal takes the
cigarette away*)
Give me one.

SUSAN
Hal, that's utter torture
for George.

(*Harry goes back to the
garage. Helen mumbles
to herself as she cleans
up the kitchen.*)

HELEN
I don't know.

GEORGE
Give me one.

HELEN
I just don't know. He used
to be so docile.

SUSAN
Don't, George. He's just
playing cat and mouse.

HELEN
And now I just don't
know—

HARRY (*calling from garage*)
Helen!

HELEN
Harry?

HAL
That's right, George.
Don't have one. I'm just
playing cat and mouse.
(*lights a cigarette*)

HARRY
Helen, my experiments.

HELEN
Harry, what?

GEORGE
Just give it to me, will
you?

HARRY
A terrible mistake.

SUSAN
Try to control yourself for
just another half hour,
George.

HELEN
Harry, your voice—

GEORGE
No.

SUSAN
Why not?

HARRY (*his voice getting
lower and gruffer*)
For the love of heaven,
Helen, keep away from
me.

GEORGE

Because I don't wanna
control myself for just
another half hour.

HAL

Whatever you want,
George.
(*hands a cigarette to
George*)

HELEN

What happened?

HARRY

I can't restrain myself anymore. I'm coming through
the garage door.
(*comes through the ga-
rage door, wearing a
monster mask; his voice
is now very deep and
gruff*)
I'm irresistibly attracted
to you, Helen, irresistibly.

HELEN

Eeeeeeeeeeeeeeeeeeeeeek!

HARRY (*stepping toward her*)
Helen, I love you.
(*goes to embrace her*)

HELEN

Harry, you're hideous.
Eeeeek! Eeeeeeeeeeeek!
Eeeeeeeeeeeeek!

(*As Helen screams, Wonderboy is discovered, in mufti, doing his homework.*)

SUSAN

What was the point of that, Hal?

HAL

No point.

WONDERBOY

Two superquantums plus five uranium neutrons, and I've got the mini-sub fuel. Hooray. Boy, will my friends in the U.S. Navy be pleased. Hey, what's that? Better use my wonder-vision. Helen Fargis seems to be in trouble. Better change to Wonderboy.

(*as if throwing open his shirt*)

And fly over there in a flash.

(*jumping as if flying*)

I guess I'm in the nick of time.

(*with one super-powerful punch in the jaw he subdues Harry, the monster*)

HELEN

Oh, Wonderboy, what would have happened if you hadn't come? But what will happen to IT?

WONDERBOY

I'll fly him to a distant zoo where they'll take good care of him.

HELEN

Oh, Wonderboy, how can I ever repay you?

WONDERBOY

Are those home-baked cookies I smell?

SUSAN

The president of the company has an Eames chair.

(*Helen smiles at Wonderboy through her tears; he puts his arm around her shoulders.*)

WONDERBOY

Tune in tomorrow, boys and girls, when I'll subdue a whole country full of monsters.

GEORGE

How do you know that?

(*Slide: "Winners Eat Wondrex."*)

SUSAN
Jennifer showed it to me.

GEORGE
You asked to see it?

SUSAN
Don't worry George. He wasn't there. I just had this crazy wild impulse as I was passing his office. I wanted to see what it looked like. Isn't that wild?

WONDERBOY
And in the meantime, re-member: winners eat Wondrex.
(*smiles and jumps in the air, as if flying away*)

(*Slide: little girls with shopping bags.*)

FIRST NEWS ANNOUNCER
Little girls with big shopping bags means back to school season is here again. Among the many shoppers in downtown New York were Darlene, nine, Lila, four, and Lucy Gladden, seven, of Lynbrook, Long Island.

(*Slide: the Vice President.*)

FIRST NEWS ANNOUNCER
In Washington, D.C., as he left John Foster Dulles Airport, as President Johnson's favorite

HAL
Did you sit in it?

(*Slide: second view of the Vice President.*)

SUSAN

I didn't dare. What would I have said if he'd come in?

(*George goes to the rest room.*)

HAL

I love you, Mr. President of my great big company, and that's why I'm sitting in your nice warm leather arm chair.

SUSAN

You're perverted. I don't want to be a person working in a company who's never seen her president.

FIRST NEWS ANNOUNCER

representative, the Vice President said he was bursting with confidence.

(*Slide: first view of Vietnamese mourners.*)

SECOND NEWS ANNOUNCER

U.S. spokesmen in Saigon said families would be given adequate shelter and compensation. Our planes are under strict orders not to return to base with any bombs. The United States regrets that a friendly village was hit. The native toll was estimated at sixty.

SUSAN (*to Hal, who has gotten up*)
  While you're up—

(*Slide: second view of Vietnamese mourners.*)

HAL
  What?

SUSAN
  You know. Get me a Coke.
  (*titters at her own joke*)

  (*Hal goes out through the hall door. George returns from the rest room.*)

SECOND NEWS ANNOUNCER
This was high, explained spokesmen, in answer to questions, because of the type of bomb dropped. These are known as Lazy Dogs. Each Lazy Dog bomb contains ten thousand slivers of razor-sharp steel.

(*Slide: third view of Vietnamese mourners.*)

GEORGE (*turning TV sound off*)
  Can I come over tonight?

(*Volume off.*)

(*Slide: a pack of Longford cigarettes superimposed on a lake.*)

SUSAN
  Not tonight.
      (*goes to bulletin board*)

GEORGE (*following her*)
  Why not tonight?

SUSAN
  Because I don't feel like
  it.

GEORGE
  You have a date?

SUSAN
  What business is that of
  yours? Don't think be-
  cause—

GEORGE
  Who with?

SUSAN
  None of your business.

GEORGE
  What about late, after
  you get back, like one
  o'clock?

(*Two People On Tele-
vision do a silent com-
mercial for Longford
cigarettes: a man lights
a woman's cigarette and
she looks pleased.*)

SUSAN
  That's too late. I need
  lots of sleep.

GEORGE
  I'll call first.

SUSAN
  You'd better.

> (*Whenever Hal, Susan,
> and George have noth-
> ing else to do, they stare
> straight ahead, as if at
> a television screen.
> George and Susan do
> this now. Hal comes
> back with two Cokes.
> George goes to the tele-
> phone and dials it.*)

> (*Slide on the screen:
> "The Endless Fron-
> tier."*)

GEORGE
  Hello, dear. Yes, I'm here.
  Listen, I'm afraid I have
  to take the midnight to
  three shift.

> (*Sally and Bill are two
> characters in the West-
> ern.*)

> (*Hal turns TV volume
> on.*)

SALLY
  Don't go, Bill.

BILL
I've got to.

GEORGE
I've got to. The night su-
pervisor is out.

SALLY
Oh, Bill.

GEORGE
And I've already said I
would.

(*Bill leaves.*)

SALLY
Oh, Bill.

GEORGE
Listen, let's talk about it
over dinner, huh? I'll be
out after you go to sleep
and in before you wake
up so what's the differ-
ence? Listen, let's talk
about it over dinner, I
said. Listen, I love you.
Goodbye.
(*hangs up*)

(*Sally fixes her hair in
the mirror.*)

HAL (*watching TV intently
but talking to George*)
You have to take the mid-
night to three shift,
George? That's really too
bad.

(*Sally is surprised by
Steve, the villain, who
has just been waiting
for Bill to ride off.*)

SALLY
Steve!

HAL
Got a call while I was out?

STEVE
Bill's dead, Sally.

SALLY
I don't believe you.

GEORGE (*snapping TV volume off*)
Do either of you want to take on some evening overtime this week?

(*Volume off.*)

(*Steve tries to embrace Sally. She slaps him hard as he approaches her. He tries it again. She slaps him again. He tries it a third time. She gets him a third time. Then he grabs and kisses her despite her terrible struggling.*)

SUSAN
Which?

GEORGE
Five to midnight Tuesday and Thursday.

HAL
Thursday.

SUSAN
Oh, all right, I'll take Tuesday.

HAL
Did you want Thursday?

SUSAN
I'd like to get the apartment finished.

HAL
> Then give me Tuesday.

SUSAN
> Not if you HAVE something on Thursday.

HAL
> No sweat.

SUSAN
> Oh, I know. It was that talk with that man.

> (*Hal turns TV volume on.*)

GEORGE (*snapping TV volume off*)
> What talk with what man?

SUSAN
> A man he has to talk to.

GEORGE
> About a job?

HAL
> I probably won't even see him.

> (*Bill, his arm wounded, appears again. Seeing Steve with Sally, he draws and aims.*)

BILL
> Sally, duck!

> (*Volume off.*)

> (*Sally ducks. Bill shoots Steve, then goes to Sally to make sure she's all right. Steve, however, is not badly wounded and he reaches for Bill's gun. The gun falls to the floor and they fight. Sally tries to get into the fight, but is pushed away.*)

GEORGE
What kind of job?

HAL
For the government. I tell
you I probably won't see
him.

GEORGE
If you quit, Hal, I'll need
three weeks' notice. If you
care about severance pay.

HAL (*turning TV volume
on*)
I haven't seen him yet,
even.

(*Bill is losing his fight
with Steve because of
his wounded arm. Steve
is about to get the gun.*)

GEORGE
Or about me.

SALLY (*warningly*)
Bill!

HAL
I wasn't going to mention
it.

SUSAN
I'm sorry. It was my fault.

GEORGE (*turning volume off*)
Just don't spring anything
on me If you don't like
the job, leave. But don't
spring anything on me

(*Volume off.*)

(*In the nick of time,
Sally shoots Steve in the
back with a rifle. As he*

because I can't take it,
you know that.

*falls he makes a mute
appeal to her. He is
dead now and she is ap-
palled at what she's
done.*)

HAL

George, I'm NOT quitting.

SUSAN

He likes this job too
much, George.

HAL

I love it more than my
own life. I wouldn't leave
it for all the world. Honest Injun, George.
        (*turns volume on*)

SALLY (*embracing Bill*)
Oh, Bill!

GEORGE

Can you imagine what I'd
have to go through to
train another person? Can
you?

BILL

I love you, Sally.

SALLY (*touched*)
Oh, Bill.

BILL

Let's move to another
town.

SALLY (*delighted*)
Oh Bill.

(*Bill and Sally ride off together into the dusk.*)

SUSAN
Listen, I just remembered a joke. There's this writing on the subway. "I love grills" it says on the wall. So somebody crosses out "grills" and writes in "girls." "I love girls" it says now. And then somebody else writes in, "What about us grills?"
(*laughs and laughs over this*)

(*Slide: the President and his family.*)

SECOND NEWS ANNOUNCER
The President is accompanied by his wife, Lady Bird Johnson, and by his two daughters, Lynda Bird Johnson and Luci Baines Johnson Nugent, who lives in nearby Austin with her husband Patrick Nugent, President Johnson's son-in-law.

SUSAN
What about us grills? Isn't that fantastic?

(*Slide: second view of the President and his family.*)

(*The President appears at a podium reading a speech. He is indeed accompanied by his wife and daughters.*)

(*Slide: the President alone.*)

HAL
What's the matter with you?

SUSAN (*still laughing*)
I think that's the funniest thing I ever heard.

HAL
Shhhh.

PRESIDENT
We will stamp out aggression wherever and whenever.

(*Susan continues laughing.*)

HAL
Shhhhh. Stop it.

SUSAN
I can't.

PRESIDENT
We will tighten our defenses and fight, to guarantee the peace of our children, our children's children, and their children.

SUSAN
I can't stop. Get the wa-
ter.

(George gets up to get
some water. Hal wants
to watch TV and can't
hear it at all because of
Susan's laughter.)

PRESIDENT
That all men are not well-
intentioned or well-in-
formed or even basically
good, is unfortunate.

HAL
This is easier.
(slaps Susan very hard
on the face)

SUSAN
Ow!

PRESIDENT
But these people will not
be indulged.

SUSAN
Just who do you think you
are!

(Applause by the Presi-
dent's family. No sound
in this play need be put
on tape; all of it can be
provided by the People
On Television.)

HAL
Are you finished?

SUSAN
I couldn't help it.

PRESIDENT
Those who are our friends
will declare themselves
publicly. The others, we
will not tolerate.

SUSAN
Sadist.

(*Slide: second view of
the President alone.*)

PRESIDENT
Belief in American success
and victory is the corner-
stone of our faith.

SUSAN
Why didn't anyone get
water?

GEORGE
Don't look at me.

PRESIDENT
Whatever else may chance
to happen on far-off
shores, nothing, I repeat
nothing, will be allowed
to disturb the serenity of
our cities and suburbs,
and when we fight we
fight for a safer and more
comfortable America, now
and in years to come.
Thank you.

SUSAN

You don't slap people be-
cause they're sick.

HAL

Every day we go through
the same thing. You
laugh. We bring you wa-
ter. You spill the water all
over everybody, and half
an hour later you stop.

SUSAN

Give me the water,
George. I'm going to take
a pill.

GEORGE

What makes you laugh
like that?

(*Hal lowers the volume
but does not turn it
off.*)

(*Slide: third view of the
President and his fam-
ily.*)

SECOND NEWS ANNOUNCER

The President and his
family will now be cheered
by the cadet corps.

(*The President and his
family respond to cheers
like mechanical dolls.
Turning his back, the
Second News An-
nouncer provides us
with one hummed bar
of "So Hello Lyn-
don."*)

(*A Spanish Teacher ap-
pears.*)

(*Slide: the Spanish
Teacher's face.*)

(*Volume low.*)

SUSAN
I'm a hysteric. I mean I'm
not constantly hysterical
but sometimes I get that
way. I react that way,
through my body. You're
a compulsive, Hal, a nasty
little compulsive.

HAL (*turning volume off*)
How do you know?

SUSAN
I've discussed it with my
analyst. Hysterics react
through their bodies.
Compulsives react com-
pulsively.

GEORGE
What does he say about
me?

SUSAN
He doesn't.

GEORGE
Hmph.

HAL
How long have you been
going now? Twenty-seven
years?

SPANISH TEACHER
Buenos dias muchachos
and muchachas. Hello,
boys and girls. Mucha-
chos. Boys. Muchachas.
Girls. Aqui es la casa.
Here is the house. Casa.
House.

(*Volume off.*)

(*The Spanish Teacher
finishes the lesson.*)

(*Efficient researchers
walk back and forth
across the stage, check-
ing things, nodding at
each other curtly, and
so on.*)

(*Slide: the efficient researchers.*)

SUSAN
> A year, wise guy.

HAL
> How long do you expect
> to be going?

SUSAN
> It might take another two
> or three years.

GEORGE
> I know people who have
> gone for ten or twelve
> years.

HAL
> Don't you think that's a
> lot?

GEORGE
> If you need it, you need
> it. It's a sickness like any
> other sickness. It's got to
> be looked after.

HAL
> What did they do in the
> old days?

GEORGE (*turning volume up*)   (*Volume up.*)
> They stayed sick.

UGP ANNOUNCER
> Who are they? They are

a community of devotion.

(*Slide: "UGP" in very Germanic lettering.*)

UGP ANNOUNCER
Men and women whose lives are dedicated to the researching of more perfect products for you. Get the benefit of a community of devotion. Look for the letters UGP whenever you buy a car, radio, television set, or any of a thousand other products. Their tool: devotion. Their goal: perfection.

(*Slide: a civil rights demonstration.*)

SUSAN
My analyst has been going to HIS analyst for twenty-five years.

HAL
How do you know?

SUSAN
He told me.

FIRST NEWS ANNOUNCER
Three men were critically injured during a civil

rights demonstration in Montgomery, Alabama today.

GEORGE
Can you feel the tranquilizer working?

SUSAN
A little bit. I think so.

(*Slide: the* Vice President.)

FIRST NEWS ANNOUNCER
This afternoon the Vice President arrived in Honolulu. As he stepped off the plane he told newsmen things are looking up.

GEORGE
Maybe I should have one too.

(*Slide: a map of China.*)

FIRST NEWS ANNOUNCER
The Defense Department today conceded that United States aircraft may have mistakenly flown over Chinese territory last month. It regrets the incident.

SUSAN (*turning volume off.*)
Are you upset?

(*Volume off.*)

(Slide: a rock and roll group.)

(A rock and roll group is seen singing and playing.)

GEORGE
I can feel my stomach.

SUSAN *(reaching into her bag to give him a pill)*
Here.

GEORGE
I'd like some coffee.

HAL
I'd like some lunch.

SUSAN
Lunch! I'll get it.
(dashes into her coat and is almost out the door)

HAL
Hey!

SUSAN
Rare with onion and a danish. I know. So long, you guys.

HAL *(throwing his penknife into the bulletin board)*
Think she's all right?

GEORGE
People wouldn't say this
was a crazy office or anything like that.

HAL
Nope.

GEORGE
She's really a nice girl,
isn't she?

HAL (*doing calisthenics*)
Yup.

GEORGE
You like her, don't you?

HAL
Yup.

GEORGE
I mean you don't just
think she's a good lay, do
you?

HAL
What makes you think I
lay her?

GEORGE
Well, don't you?

HAL

> George, that's an old
> trick.

GEORGE

> I'm just trying to find out
> if you really like her.

HAL

> Why do you care?

GEORGE

> I feel protective.

HAL

> That's right. She's half
> your age, isn't she?

GEORGE

> Not exactly half.

HAL

> How old are you, George,
> exactly?

GEORGE

> Forty-three.

HAL (*crossing to water
     cooler*)
> Humph.

GEORGE

> What's that mean?

HAL
  I was just wondering what
  it was like to be forty-
  three.

GEORGE
  It stinks.

HAL
  That's what I thought.

GEORGE
  You'll be forty-three
  sooner than you think.

HAL
  I'll never be forty-three.

GEORGE
  Why not?

HAL   (*The rock and roll
  I don't intend to live that   group bows.*)
  long.

GEORGE   (*Slide: a group of peace
  You have something?   marchers.*)

HAL   (*A group of peace
  No. I just don't intend to   marchers appears.*)
  live that long.
     (*returns to console and
     turns volume on*)

FIRST NEWS ANNOUNCER
A group of so-called peaceniks marched down the center mall of the capital today, singing:

(*The peace marchers sing "We Shall Over-come."*)

GEORGE (*sits*)
You're probably a social-ist.

HAL
A socialist?

GEORGE
A socialist at twenty and a Republican at forty. Everybody goes through that cycle.

FIRST NEWS ANNOUNCER
One young man from New York City pre-dicted:

ONE YOUNG MAN FROM NEW YORK CITY
The Washington Monu-ment's going to burst into bloom and—

(*It is as if the sound were cut off on the word he was going to say, but we can read "Fuck" on his lips.*)

GEORGE
It's healthy.

(*Slide: Annie Kappel-hoff.*)

FIRST NEWS ANNOUNCER
A little girl, Annie Kap-pelhoff, had her own opinion:

ANNIE (*as if leading a cheer*)
Burn yourselves, not your draft cards, burn your-selves, not your draft cards—

(*The sound is cut off on Annie, too, as she continues the same cheer.*)

FIRST NEWS ANNOUNCER
Later in the day Annie was the star of her own parade. She's head-cheer-leader of Wilumet High School in Maryland. To-day Annie cheered her team on to victory, thirty to nothing, over neighbor-ing South Dearing. Annie is also an ardent supporter of the young American

Nazi party, and hopes to
become a model. And
now, a message.

(*Slide: a jar of K-F
soap-cream.*)

HAL
Are you a Republican,
George?

GEORGE
That's right.

HAL
You know I have a lot of
friends who won't even
speak to Republicans.

GEORGE
I'd rather not discuss politics.

HAL
Why not?

GEORGE
Because we probably
don't see eye to eye.

HAL
So?

FAMOUS TV PERSONALITY
Are you one of those lucky
women who has all the
time in the world?

FAMOUS TV PERSONALITY
Or are you like most of
us: busy, busy, busy all
day long with home or job
so that when evening
comes you hardly have
time to wash your face,
much less transform your-
self into the living doll
he loves.

GEORGE

So I'd rather not discuss it. And my stomach's upset.

FAMOUS TV PERSONALITY

Well then, K-F is for you. More than a soap. More than a cream. It's a soap-cream. You apply it in less time than it takes to wash your face and it leaves your skin tingling with loveliness. Try it. And for an extra super thrill, use it in the shower.

(*Slide: Lily Heaven.*)

LILY HEAVEN'S ANNOUNCER

The Lily Heaven Show, ladies and gentlemen, starring that great star of stage, screen, and television: Lily Heaven.

(*Out through imaginary curtains comes Lily Heaven, very starlike. She greets her audience in her own inimitable way. She sings a line from a popular American love song.*)

(*There is a special knock on the viewing room door.*)

HAL
What's that?

GEORGE
Nothing.

    (*George turns volume off.*)   (*Volume off.*)

                                   (*Slide: a second view of Lily Heaven.*)

HAL
What do you mean, nothing?

GEORGE (*calling*)
One minute.

HAL (*getting panicky*)
One minute until what?

    (*George turns out the lights in the viewing room.*)

HAL
I knew it. What's going on?

GEORGE (*calling*)
Okay.

HAL
Okay what? What? What?

SUSAN (*coming through the
      door with a cake with
      lighted candles on it*)
   Okay this, stupid.

HAL
   Oh my God, you're crazy.

SUSAN AND GEORGE
   One, two, three.
      (*singing*)
   Happy Birthday to you,
   Happy Birthday to you,
   Happy Birthday dear Ha-
   al,
   Happy Birthday to you.

      (*Susan kisses Hal on
      the lips.*)

SUSAN
   Happy Birthday. You had
   no idea, did you?

HAL
   No.

GEORGE
   Happy Birthday.

HAL
   Thanks a lot.

SUSAN
Make a wish and blow.

(*Hal blows on the candles but doesn't get them all.*)

SUSAN
Well, almost.

(*George turns the viewing room lights on again, and Susan gets two presents from the closet.*)

SUSAN
People thought I was crazy walking down the hall with this cake and this lunch in a paper bag. And I was petrified one of you would swing the door open while I was waiting in the corridor and knock me down and the cake and everything. I was almost sure you'd guessed, Hal, when I put the presents in my locker this morning.

HAL
I hadn't.

SUSAN

I love birthdays. I know
it's childish but I really
do. Look at the card on
George's.

HAL

It's cute.

SUSAN

Open it.

(*Hal opens the pack-
age. It's a tie.*)

HAL

Well thanks, George. I
can use this.
(*makes a mock noose
of it around his neck*)

GEORGE

You're welcome.

SUSAN (*looking at the label
as if she hadn't seen it
before*)
It's a good tie.

GEORGE

What'd you expect?

(*George is biting into
an egg salad sandwich.*

*Hal starts to open the
second present.)*

SUSAN (*stopping Hal*)
Save mine for when we
eat the cake, so the birthday will last longer.

HAL
George, there's egg salad
all over the dials.

GEORGE (*turning volume on*)
Sorry.

SUSAN
Here's a napkin. I'll make
some coffee.

GEORGE
Good.

(*Lily Heaven finishes
singing and bows.*)

LILY HEAVEN
So long, everybody.

LILY HEAVEN
This is Lily Heaven say-
ing so long.

(*Applause from part of
Lily Heaven's audience,
played by the People
On Television, who
stand behind her.*)

LILY HEAVEN (*as if each sentence were her last*)
Here's wishing you a good
week before we meet
again. From all of us here

to all of you out there: so long. Thanks a lot and God bless you. This is Lily signing off. I only hope that you enjoyed watching us as much as we enjoyed being here. So long. It's been wonderful being with you. Really grand, and I hope you'll invite us into your living room again next week. I only wish we could go on but I'm afraid it's time to say so long, so from the actors and myself, from the staff here, I want to wish you all a very very good week. This is your Lily saying so long to you. So long. So long. So long. So long. Have a happy, and so long. Till next week. Bye. So long. Bye. So long.

(George and Hal are mesmerized by Lily Heaven. Susan is paying no attention but is fussing with the coffee things and putting paper bags, as party hats, on Hal and George.)

GEORGE

Give me another of those tranquilizers, please. The first one doesn't seem to have done a thing.

(Slide: a weather map.)

WEATHER ANNOUNCER
And now, the weather.

(Hal turns the volume off. Susan has plugged in the hot plate and coffee maker. She also has some real coffee and a jar of dried cream, some sugar and sugar substitute in little bags stolen from a luncheonette, napkins and little wooden stick-stirrers.)

(*Volume off.*)

HAL (*who has been opening his present*)
Say, this is nice.

SUSAN
It's an art book.

HAL
I can see that.

GEORGE
Hal especially interested in art?

SUSAN
A person doesn't have to be especially interested in art to like it.

HAL

    It must have cost a lot,
Susan. Here, George.
    (*passes George a piece
of cake*)

SUSAN

    Well, as a matter of fact,
I got it on sale at Mar-
boro.

HAL

    If I had a place for it
everything would be fine.
Cake, Susan?

SUSAN (*to George*)

    Hal still doesn't have a
place.

    (*Slide: Miracle Head-
ache Pills.*)

GEORGE

    What kind of place are
you looking for?

    (*Still without volume,
an advertisement for
Miracle Headache Pills:
a woman is seen before
and after taking the
pills.*)

HAL

    I'd like to find an apart-
ment with more than one
small room for under a
hundred dollars.

SUSAN

    Do you want to live in the
Village?

HAL
>Makes no difference.

GEORGE
>Don't live down there.

SUSAN
>Why not?

GEORGE
>It's too crowded.

SUSAN
>It's not so crowded, and
>in the Village you can see
>a lot of wonderful faces.

GEORGE
>Yes, well frankly I've been
>working for a living for
>twenty-one years and I re-
>sent having to support a
>lot of bums on relief.

SUSAN
>That's not the Village.
>That's the Bowery.

>*(Lady Announcer be-
>gins to speak, still with-
>out volume.)*

GEORGE
>Let's not talk about it.

SUSAN
>Why not?

>*(Slide: First Federal
>Savings Bank.)*

GEORGE

I already told Hal that people with differing points of view shouldn't talk about politics. And I shouldn't be eating this cake either.

(*snaps volume on*)

LADY ANNOUNCER

And now First Federal Savings and Kennel-Heart Dog Food present Luncheon With Carol, a program especially designed for the up-to-date woman. Our topic for today: I Quit. And here's Carol.

(*Slide: Carol and Ron Campbell.*)

CAROL

Hello, ladies. This is Carol. I have as my guest today Mr. Ron Campbell just back from an eighteen month tour of duty in Vietnam. Mr. Campbell was a member of the famed Green Berets. He is a holder of the Bronze Star and the South Vietnamese Order of Merit; he has been nominated for the U.S. Silver Star. A few weeks ago he was offered a field commission as captain. But instead of accepting, what did you do, Ron?

RON
    I quit.

CAROL
    That's right, you quit.
    Tell us why you quit,
    Ron, when you were ob-
    viously doing so well.

RON
    I didn't like being there.

CAROL
    You didn't?

RON
    No.

CAROL (*cheerfully*)
    I see.

RON
    We're committing mass
    murder.

CAROL (*interested*)
    Yes?

RON
    We're trying to take over
    a people that don't want
    to be taken over by any-
    body.

CAROL
  Now, Ron, American boys
  are out there dying so
  somebody must be doing
  something wrong some-
  where.

RON
  Whoever in Hanoi or
  Peking or Washington is
  sending men out to be
  killed, THEY'RE doing
  something wrong.

CAROL (*interested in his
    opinion, tolerant*)
  I see.

RON
  You do? Well I was there
  for a year and a half and
  every day I saw things that
  would make you sick.
  Heads broken, babies
  smashed against walls—

CAROL (*deeply sympathetic*)
  I KNOW.

RON
  You know?

CAROL
  War is horrible.

RON
    Listen—

CAROL
    Thank you, Ron. We've
    been talking this after-
    noon, ladies, with Ron
    Campbell, war hero.

RON
    Will you let me say some-
    thing, please?

CAROL   (*tolerating   him,
        kindly*)
    And a fascinating talk it's
    been, Ron, but I'm afraid
    our time is up.

RON
    One—

CAROL   (*with   her   special
        smile for the ladies*)
    Ladies, see you all tomor-
    row.

SUSAN (*dreamily*)
    I think I'm floating fur-
    ther and further left.

GEORGE
    You don't know a thing
    about it.

SUSAN
I was listening to Norman
Thomas last night—

LADY ANNOUNCER
This program was brought
to you by First Federal
Savings and Kennel-Heart
Dog Food. The opinions
expressed on this program
are not necessarily those
of anyone connected with
it. A dog in the home
means a dog with a heart.

GEORGE
I'm going to the Men's
Room.

(*Slide: Kennel-Heart
Dog Food.*)

LADY ANNOUNCER
Kennel-Heart. Bow-wow.
Wow.

SUSAN
Poor George.

(*Slide: "Billion Dollar
Movie."*)

HAL
You still haven't told me
about tonight.

SUSAN
Told you what about to-
night?

(*A very English man
and a very English
woman appear in the
movie.*)

HE
Sarah.

HAL
Are we going to the mov-
ies or are we not going to
the movies?

SUSAN
I don't know. I can't make
up my mind.

HAL
That's just fine.

SUSAN
I want to work on my
apartment.

HAL
Okay.

SUSAN
I should really get it done.

SHE
Yes, Richard.

HE
Our old apartment.

SHE
Yes, Richard. It's still
here.

HE
It seems very small to me.

SHE
It does to me, too.

HE
Do you think we can live
in it again?

SHE
Not in the old way.

HAL
  You're right.

SUSAN
  Suppose I let you know
  by the end of the afternoon?

HAL
  Suppose we forget I ever
  suggested it.

HE
  In a better way.

SHE
  You've changed too, Richard, for the better.

HE
  So have you, darling, for
  the better.

SHE
  I've learned a lot.

HE
  Maybe that's what war is
  for.

    (*The People On Tele-
    vision hum "White
    Cliffs of Dover" under
    the following.*)

SHE
  The brick wall in front of
  the window is gone.

HE

We'll rebuild for the future.

SUSAN

Oh, all right, I'll go. Happy?

HAL

I'm so happy I could put a bullet through my brain.

SHE

I hope there is never any more war. Ever, ever again.

HE

Amen.

(*Slide: "The End."*)

(*The People On Television sing, meaningfully, the last line of "White Cliffs of Dover": "Tomorrow, just you wait and see."*)

SUSAN

Sugar?

HAL

You're like my grandmother.

(*First News Announcer appears.*)

SUSAN
How?

HAL
She asked me if I took sugar every day we lived together. It was very comforting.

(*Slide: baseball player.*)

FIRST NEWS ANNOUNCER
Baseball's Greg Pironelli, fifty-six, died today of a heart attack in St. Petersburg, Florida. He hit a total of four hundred and eighty home runs and had a lifetime batting average of three forty-one.

HAL
Hal, she used to say to me, my grandmother, you're going to be a big man.

HAL
Everybody's going to love you. She used to sing that song to me: "Poppa's gonna buy you a dog named Rover, and if that dog don't bark, Poppa's gonna buy you a looking glass, and if that looking glass should break, you're still the sweetest little boy in town."

(*Slide: a baseball game.*)

FIRST NEWS ANNOUNCER
In 1963, the year he was elected to baseball's hall of fame in Cooperstown, New York, Pironelli suffered his first stroke. Pironelli owned a Florida-wide chain of laundries.

(*Slide: "Johnny Holland Show."*)

JOHNNY
We're back.

(*Slide: Johnny and Luci.*)

SUSAN
That's nice.

JOHNNY
That's a very pretty dress you've got on, Luci.

(*George enters and goes directly to telephone.*)

LUCI
Thank you, Johnny.

GEORGE
Hello, darling? Listen, I've gotten out of it. Isn't that good news? The midnight shift.

JOHNNY
How does it feel living in Austin after all the excitement of the big wedding?

LUCI
It feels fine.

GEORGE
I'm looking forward to being home nice and comfy with you.

JOHNNY
Do you miss your father?

GEORGE
You know my stomach is killing me. Sure I will. Wait a minute.

LUCI
Oh sure, I miss him.

(*George takes out a
pencil.*)

GEORGE
Toothpaste. Cauliflower.
That's a good idea.

JOHNNY (*awkward pause*)
I guess your heart belongs
to Daddy, huh?

GEORGE
Large face cream. Why
large? No, I don't care. I
was just asking.

LUCI
That's right.

JOHNNY (*awkward pause*)
Is your father hard to get
along with?

GEORGE
Okay. Listen, I'm really
looking forward to seeing
you.

LUCI
Oh, no. When I want
something I just march
right in, cuddle up in his
lap, and give him a great
big kiss.

(*Slide: a second view of
Johnny and Luci.*)

JOHNNY (*awkward pause*)
So you'd say your father is
affectionate?

LUCI
Very affectionate.

GEORGE
No, I haven't been drink-
ing, and it's rotten of you
to ask.

JOHNNY (*awkward pause*)
Does he ever ask your ad-
vice about important mat-
ters?

GEORGE
Okay, okay. Bye.
(*hangs up telephone*)

LUCI
Well, one day I told him
what I thought, good and
proper, about all those
nervous nellies interfering
with my Daddy's war.

(*Johnny does a double
take of scandalized
amusement to the au-
dience.*)

(*Slide: Johnny doing
double take.*)

JOHNNY
And what did he say?

LUCI
He laughed.

SUSAN
Have a little coffee,
George.

GEORGE
No, thanks.

HAL
Oh, come on, George,
have a little coffee.

GEORGE
A sip.

JOHNNY
It's lovely talking to you,
Luci.

SUSAN
Sugar or superine?

LUCI
It's nice talking to you
too, Johnny.

GEORGE
Sugar.

JOHNNY
We'll be back.

SUSAN
George.

(*Slide: "Johnny Holland Show."*)

GEORGE
Don't take care of me. I
said sugar.

SUSAN
Whatever   you   want,
George.

*(An Evangelist appears
with his choir, which is
singing "Onward Chris-
tian Soldiers.")*

(Slide: the Evangelist.)

EVANGELIST
If we could look through
the ceiling of this wonderful new air-conditioned
stadium we could see the
stars. Nonetheless I have
heard them in faraway
countries, I have heard
them criticize, criticize us
and the leaders we know
and love.

SUSAN
George, what are you eat-
ing now?

GEORGE
Chicken sandwich.

SUSAN
Give me a bite.

*(Hal plays with his pen-
knife. Susan eats an-
other piece of cake.
George eats his chicken
sandwich.)*

EVANGELIST
Why? Well I will tell you
why. They criticize us because we are rich, as if
money itself were evil.
Money, the Bible says, is
the root of evil, not evil
itself. I have seen a room-

ful of men and women, powerful Hollywood celebrities at four o'clock A.M. in the morning, listening to me with tears streaming down their faces crying out to me that they had lost touch with God.

(*George starts to cough.*)

EVANGELIST
"In God We Trust" is on our coins, ladies and gentlemen—

 (*Slide: a second view of the Evangelist.*)

SUSAN
What's the matter, George?

 (*The evangelist choir sings "Onward Christian Soldiers."*)

(*George motions her away and continues to cough.*)

HAL (*turning volume off*)
Spit it out, George.

(*Volume off.*)

SUSAN
Hal, leave him alone.

HAL

    George, spit it out.
      (*thumps George on the
      back*)

SUSAN

    Hal! George, is it epi-
    lepsy?

HAL

    It's something in his
    throat.

SUSAN

    Try to tell us what it is,
    George.

HAL AND GEORGE
    Chicken!

HAL

    He has a chicken bone
    stuck in his throat.

SUSAN

    Oh my God. Well give
    him some water.

      (*George's choking is
      getting worse.*)

HAL

    Water will wash right by
    it. Let me look.

> (*holds George's head
> and looks into his
> mouth*)

Don't move, George. I
want to take a look.
> (*looks in George's
> mouth*)

There it is.

SUSAN (*also looking*)
Ugh, it's stuck in his
throat. I'll get some wa-
ter.

> (*Hal and Susan let go
> of George, who falls to
> the floor.*)

HAL
Not water.

SUSAN
Why not?

HAL
Because water will wash
right past the thing. It
needs something to push
it out.

SUSAN
Like what?

HAL

Like bread.

SUSAN

Bread? Bread will get
stuck on the bone and
he'll choke.

HAL

You're wrong.

SUSAN

I'm right.

HAL

Bread will push it right
down.

SUSAN

Water will do that.

HAL

You're wrong.

SUSAN

It's you that's wrong and
won't admit it.

HAL

I'm going to give him
some bread.

SUSAN

I won't allow it.

HAL
YOU won't allow it?

SUSAN
It'll kill him.

HAL
He's choking right now
and I'm going to give him
some of this bread.

SUSAN
Give him water.

HAL
I said bread.

SUSAN (*starting to walk past
    Hal*)
And I said water.

HAL (*grabbing her arm*)
Bread.

SUSAN
Water. Ow, you're hurt-
ing me.

(*George is having a
very bad time. Hal and
Susan turn to look at
him, speaking softly.*)

SUSAN
> Let's call the operator.

HAL
> It would take too long.

SUSAN
> And he wouldn't like any-
> one to see him.

HAL
> Why not?

SUSAN
> I don't know.

> *(At this point George
> finally coughs the thing
> up, and his cough sub-
> sides into an animal
> pant.)*

SUSAN *(going to him, pat-
> ting him)*
> Poor George.

HAL
> It's over.

SUSAN
> No thanks to you.

HAL
>Nor you.

SUSAN (*putting George's head on her breast*)
>He might have choked. Poor George.

GEORGE (*pushing her away*)
>Fuck!

>>(*George lurches against the console on his way to the bathroom, accidentally turning on the volume.*)

EVANGELIST CHOIR (*still singing "Onward Christian Soldiers."*)
>"With the cross of Jesus—"

>(*Hal changes channels from the Evangelist's meeting to "My Favorite Teenager."*)

>(*Slide: Mother, Father, and Daughter in "My Favorite Teenager."*)

SUSAN (*sitting in her chair*)
>Poor George.

MOTHER
>Why aren't you going?

DAUGHTER (*sitting in George's chair at the control console*)

Because I told Harold
Sternpepper he could take
me.

MOTHER
Yes, and—

DAUGHTER
Well, Harold Sternpepper
is a creep. Everybody
knows that.

(*The remaining People
On Television make the
sound of canned laugh-
ter.*)

HAL (*sitting in his chair*)
What movie are we going
to?

MOTHER
So, why—

DAUGHTER
Oh, because I was mad at
Gail.

(*Canned laughter.*)

SUSAN
I don't know.

MOTHER
What about Johnny Beau-
mont?

HAL
  What about George?

SUSAN
  What about him?
	DAUGHTER
	  What about him?

HAL
  Well, I guess it's none of
  my business.
	MOTHER
	  Well, I guess it's none of
	  my business.

GEORGE (*returning*)
  What's the matter?
	FATHER
	  What's the matter?

	(*Slide: second view of
	  Mother, Father, and
	  Daughter in "My Fa-
	  vorite Teenager."*)

SUSAN
  Nothing.
	DAUGHTER
	  Nothing.

GEORGE
  Going somewhere?
	FATHER
	  Why aren't you dressed
	  for the prom?

	DAUGHTER
	  I'm not going to the
	  prom.

SUSAN
  We're going to the mov-
  ies.	

	FATHER
	  Why not? Why isn't she
	  going, Grace?

(*Hal and Susan and George are slowing down because they are mesmerized by "My Favorite Teenager."*)

GEORGE
What movie are you going to?

GEORGE
Mind if I come along?

SUSAN
Oh, George, you don't really want to.

GEORGE
I'd be pleased as punch.

MOTHER
Don't ask me. I just live here.

(*Canned laughter.*)

FATHER
Why doesn't anybody tell me anything around here?

(*Canned laughter.*)

DAUGHTER (*getting up from George's chair*)
Oh, why don't you two leave me alone? I'm not going because nobody's taking me.

FATHER (*sitting in George's chair*)
Nobody's taking my little girl to the junior prom? I'll take her myself.

DAUGHTER (*stifling a yelp of horror*)
Oh no, Daddy, don't bother. I mean how would it look, I mean—

FATHER
I'd be pleased as punch.

DAUGHTER (*aside to Mother*)
Help.

(*Canned laughter.*)

SUSAN
Hal, say something.

MOTHER (*to Father*)
Now, dear, don't you
think for your age—

(*Canned laughter.*)

HAL (*to George*)
You look bushed to me,
George.

GEORGE
Who's bushed?

FATHER
My age?

(*Canned laughter.*)

FATHER (*standing and doing
a two-step*)
I'd like to see anybody
laugh at my two-step.

(*George sits in his
chair.*)

(*Canned laughter.*)

DAUGHTER (*in despair*)
Oh, Daddy. Mother, DO
something.

(*Hal, Susan, and
George are completely
mesmerized by the TV
show.*)

(*Canned laughter.*)

MOTHER (*putting her arm
around George's shoul-
ders*)

I think it's a very nice
idea. And maybe I'll go
with Harold Sternpepper.

(*Canned laughter.*)

DAUGHTER (*loudly, sitting on
Hal's knee*)
Oh, Mother, oh, Daddy,
oh no!

(*The canned laughter
mounts. Music.*)

(*Slide: "My Favorite
Teenager."*)

(*Now they all speak like situation-comedy characters.*)

HAL
What movie shall we go
to?

GEORGE
Let's talk about it over
dinner.

HAL
Who said anything about
dinner?

(*All of the People On
Television do canned
laughter now. They are
crowded around the
control console.*)

SUSAN

    Isn't anybody going to ask
me what I want to do?

                                (Canned laughter.)

GEORGE

    Sure, what do you want,
Susan?

HAL

    It's up to you.

                                  *(Slide: Hal, Susan, and
George with the same
facial expressions they
now have on the stage.)*

SUSAN

    Well, have I got a surprise
for you two. I'M going
home to fix up my apart-
ment and you two can
have dinner TOGETHER.

    *(Hal, Susan, and George join in the canned laughter.
Then, lights off. Slide off. Curtain call: all are in the
same position, silent, their faces frozen into laughing
masks.)*

MOTEL

A Masque for Three Dolls

... after all our subtle colour and nervous rhythm, after the
faint mixed tints of Conder, what more is possible? After us
the Savage God.

W.B. Yeats

MOTEL (under the title AMERICA HURRAH) was first presented at the Cafe La Mama, in the spring of 1965, directed
by Michael Kahn.

The actors in the dolls in the 1966 Pocket Theatre production:

Motel-Keeper	Brenda Smiley
Man	Conard Fowkes
Woman	James Barbosa

Motel-Keeper's Voice: Ruth White

Music: Marianne de Pury

> Lights come up on the Motel-Keeper doll. The intensity
> of the light will increase as the play continues.

> The Motel-Keeper doll is large, much larger than human
> size, but the impression of hugeness can come mainly
> from the fact that her head is at least three times larger
> than would be normal in proportion to her body. She is

all gray. She has a large full skirt which reaches to the floor. She has squarish breasts. The hair curlers on her head suggest electronic receivers.

The Motel-Keeper doll has eyeglasses which are mirrors. It doesn't matter what these mirrors reflect at any given moment. The audience may occasionally catch a glimpse of itself, or be bothered by reflections of light in the mirrors. It doesn't matter; the sensory nerves of the audience are not to be spared.

The motel room in which the Motel-Keeper doll stands is anonymously modern, except for certain "homey" touches. A neon light blinks outside the window. The colors in the room, like the colors in the clothes on the Man and Woman dolls, are violent combinations of oranges, pinks, and reds against a reflective plastic background.

The Motel-Keeper's Voice, which never stops, comes from a loudspeaker, or from several loudspeakers in the theatre. The Voice will be, at first, mellow and husky and then, as the light grows harsher and brighter, the Voice will grow harsher too, more set in its pattern, hard finally, and patronizing and petty.

An actor on platform shoes works the Motel-Keeper doll from inside it. The actor can move only the doll's arms or its entire body. As the Voice begins, the arms move, and then the Motel-Keeper doll fusses about the room in little circles.

MOTEL-KEEPER'S VOICE.   I am old. I am an old idea: the walls; that from which it springs forth. I enclose the nothing, making then a place in which it happens. I am the room: a Roman theatre where cheers break loose the lion; a railroad carriage in the forest at Compiègne, in 1918, and in 1941. I have been rooms of marble and rooms of cork, all letting forth an avalanche. Rooms of mud and rooms of silk. This room will be slashed too, as if by a scimitar, its contents spewed and yawned out. That is what happens. It is almost happening, in fact. I am this room.

(*As the Motel-Keeper's Voice continues, the doors at the back of the room open and headlights shine into the eyes of the audience; passing in front of the headlights, in silhouette, we see two more huge dolls, the Man and the Woman.*)

MOTEL-KEEPER'S VOICE.   It's nice; not so fancy as some, but with all the conveniences. And a touch of home. The antimacassar comes from my mother's house in Boise. Boise, Idaho. Sits kind of nice, I think, on the Swedish swing. That's my own idea, you know. All modern, up-to-date, that's it—no motel on this route is more up-to-date. Or cleaner. Go look, then talk me a thing or two.

(*The Woman doll enters. Her shoulders are thrown way back, like a girl posing for a calendar. Her breasts are particularly large and perfect, wiggleable if possible. She has a cherry-lipstick smile, blond hair, and a garish patterned dress.*

Both the Man and the Woman dolls are the same size as the Motel-Keeper doll, with heads at least three times larger than would be normal for their bodies. The Man and the Woman dolls, however, are flesh-colored and have more mobility. The actors inside these dolls are also on platform shoes. There is absolutely no rapport between the Motel-Keeper and the Man and Woman. All of the Motel-Keeper's remarks are addressed generally. She is never directly motivated by the actions of the Man and Woman dolls.

As the Woman doll enters, she puts down her purse and inspects the room. Then she takes off her dress, revealing lace panties and bra.)

MOTEL-KEEPER'S VOICE.   All modern here but, as I say, with the tang of home. Do you understand? When folks are fatigued, in a strange place? Not that it's old-fashioned. No. Not in the wrong way. There's a push-button here for TV. The toilet flushes of its own accord. All you've got to do is get off. Pardon my mentioning it, but you'll have to go far before you see a thing like that on this route. Oh, it's quite a room. Yes. And reasonable. Sign here. Pardon the pen leak. I can see you're fatigued.

(The Woman doll goes into the bathroom.)

MOTEL-KEEPER'S VOICE.   Any children? Well, that's nice. Children don't appreciate travel. And rooms don't appreciate children. As it happens it's the last one I've got left. I'll just flip my vacancy switch. Twelve dollars, please. In advance that'll be. That way you can go any time you want to go, you know, get an early start. On a trip to see sights, are you? That's nice. You just get your luggage while I unlock the room. You can see the light.

(The Man doll enters carrying a suitcase. He has a cigar and a loud Florida shirt. He closes the door, inspects the

room, and takes off his clothes, except for his loudly pat-
terned shorts.)

MOTEL-KEEPER'S VOICE.   There now. What I say doesn't matter. You can see. It speaks for itself. The room speaks for
itself. You can see it's a perfect 1966 room. But a taste of
home. I've seen to that. A taste of home.
Comfy, cozy, nice, but a taste of newness. That's what.
You can see it.
The best stop on route Six Sixty-Six. Well, there might be
others like it, but this is the best stop. You've arrived at the
right place. This place. And a hooked rug. I don't care
what, but I've said no room IS without a hooked rug.

(*Sound of the toilet flushing.*)

MOTEL-KEEPER'S VOICE.   No complaints yet. Never. Modern
people like modern places. Oh yes. I can tell. They tell me.
And reasonable. Very very reasonable rates. No cheaper
rates on the route, not for this. You receive what you pay
for.

(*Sound of the toilet flushing again.*)

MOTEL-KEEPER'S VOICE.   All that driving and driving and driving. Fatigued. You must be. I would be. Miles and miles
and miles.

(*The Man doll begins an inspection of the bed. He pulls
at the bedspread, testing its strength.*)

MOTEL-KEEPER'S VOICE.   Fancy. Fancy your ending up right
here. You didn't know and I didn't know. But you did. End

up right here. Respectable and decent and homelike. Right here.

(*The Woman doll comes back from the bathroom to get her negligee from her purse. She returns to the bathroom.*)

MOTEL-KEEPER'S VOICE. All folks everywhere sitting in the very palm of God. Waiting, whither, whence.

(*The Man doll pulls the bedspread, blankets, and sheets off the bed, tearing them apart. He jumps hard on the bed.*)

MOTEL-KEEPER'S VOICE. Any motel you might have come to on Six Sixty-Six. Any motel. On that vast network of roads Whizzing by, whizzing by. Trucks too. And cars from everywhere. Full up with folks, all sitting in the very palm of God. I can tell proper folks when I get a look at them. All folks.

(*The Man doll rummages through the suitcase, throwing clothes about the room.*)

MOTEL-KEEPER'S VOICE. Country roads, state roads, United States roads. It's a big world and here you are. I noticed you got a license plate. I've not been to there myself. I've not been to anywhere myself, excepting town for supplies, and Boise. Boise, Idaho.

(*Toilet articles and bathroom fixtures, including toilet paper and the toilet seat, are thrown out of the bath-*

room. The Man doll casually tears pages out of the Bible.)

MOTEL-KEEPER'S VOICE.   The world arrives to me, you'd say. It's a small world. These plastic flowers here: "Made in Japan" on the label. You noticed? Got them from the catalogue. Cat-al-ogue. Every product in this room is ordered.

(The Man doll pulls down some of the curtains. Objects continue to be thrown from the bathroom.)

MOTEL-KEEPER'S VOICE.   Ordered from the catalogue. Excepting the antimacassars and the hooked rug. Made the hooked rug myself. Tang of home. No room is a room without. Course the bedspread, hand-hooked, hooked near here at town. Mrs. Harritt. Betsy Harritt gets materials through another catalogue. Cat-al-ogue.

(The Woman doll comes out of the bathroom wearing her negligee over her panties and bra. When the Man doll notices her, he stops his other activities and goes to her.)

MOTEL-KEEPER'S VOICE.   Myself, I know it from the catalogue: bottles, bras, breakfasts, refrigerators, cast iron gates, plastic posies,

(The Woman doll opens her negligee and the Man doll pulls off her bra. The Man and Woman dolls embrace. The Woman doll puts lipstick on her nipples.)

MOTEL-KEEPER'S VOICE.   paper subscriptions, Buick trucks, blankets, forks, clitter-clack darning hooks, transistors and antimacassar, vinyl plastics,

(The Man doll turns on the TV. It glares viciously and plays loud rock and roll music.)

MOTEL-KEEPER'S VOICE.   crazy quilts, paper hairpins, cats, catnip, club feet, canisters, banisters, holy books, tattooed toilet articles, tables, tea cozies,

(The Man doll writes simple obscene words on the wall. The Woman doll does the same with her lipstick.)

MOTEL-KEEPER'S VOICE.   pickles, bayberry candles, South Dakotan Kewpie Dolls, fiberglass hair, polished milk, amiable grandpappies, colts, Galsworthy books, cribs, cabinets, teeter-totters,

(The Woman doll has turned to picture-making. She draws a crude cock and coyly adds pubic hair and drops of come.)

MOTEL-KEEPER'S VOICE.   and television sets.
Oh I tell you it, I do. It's a wonder. Full with things, the world, full up. Shall I tell you my thought? Next year there's a shelter to be built by me, yes. Shelter motel. Everything to be placed under the ground. Signs up in every direction up and down Six Sixty-Six.

(The Man and Woman dolls twist.)

MOTEL-KEEPER'S VOICE.   Complete Security, Security While You Sleep Tight, Bury Your Troubles At This Motel, Homelike, Very Comfy, and Encased In Lead, Every Room Its Own Set, Fourteen Day Emergency Supplies $5.00 Extra,

(The rock and roll music gets louder and louder. A civil-defense siren, one long wail, begins to build. The Man

*and Woman dolls proceed methodically to greater and
greater violence. They smash the TV screen and picture
frames. They pull down the remaining curtains, smash
the window, throw bits of clothing and bedding around,
and finally tear off the arms of the Motel-Keeper doll.)*

MOTEL-KEEPER'S VOICE. Self-Contained Latrine Waters, Fil-
ters, Counters, Periscopes and Mechanical Doves, Hooked
Rugs, Dearest Little Picture Frames for Loved Ones—Made
in Japan—through the catalogue. Cat-a-logue. You can pick
items and products: cablecackles—so nice—cuticles, twice-
twisted combs with corrugated calisthenics, meat-beaters,
fish-tackles, bug bombs, toasted terra-cotta'd Tanganyikan
switch blades, ochre closets, ping-pong balls, didies, Capri-
corn and Cancer prognostics, crackers, total uppers, stick
pins, basting tacks . . .

*(The Motel-Keeper's Voice is drowned out by the other
sounds—siren and music—which have built to a deafening pitch and come from all parts of the theatre. The
door opens again and headlights shine into the eyes of
the audience.*

*The actor inside the Motel-Keeper doll has slipped out
of it. The Man and Woman dolls tear off the head of
the Motel-Keeper doll, then throw her body aside.*

*Then, one by one, the Man and Woman dolls leave the
motel room and walk down the aisle. Fans blow air
through the debacle on stage onto the audience.*

*After an instant more of excruciatingly loud noise: black-
out and silence.*

*It is preferable that the actors take no bow after this
play.)*

THE SERPENT

A Ceremony

To the memory of Roger H. Klein

THE SERPENT, *a ceremony created by the Open Theater under the direction of* JOSEPH CHAIKIN, *assisted by* ROBERTA SKLAR, *words and structure by* JEAN-CLAUDE VAN ITALLIE, *opened in Rome at the Teatro del Arte on May 2, 1968.*

The Open Theater company of actors:

JOYCE AARON	JAYNE HAYNES
JAMES BARBOSA	RALPH LEE
RAYMOND BARRY	DOROTHY LYMAN
JENN BEN-YAKOV	PETER MALONEY
SHAMI CHAIKIN	ELLEN SCHINDLER
BRENDA DIXON	TINA SHEPARD
RON FABER	BARBARA VANN
CYNTHIA HARRIS	LEE WORLEY
PHILIP HARRIS	PAUL ZIMET

The arrangers of sounds: STANLEY WALDEN *and* RICHARD PEASLEE

Associate: PATRICIA COOPER

The stage manager: KEN GLICKFELD

The administrative director: RICHARD SNYDER

Costumes by: GWEN FABRICANT

5

Theater is not electronic. Unlike movies and unlike television, it does require the live presence of both audience and actors in a single space. This is the theater's uniquely important advantage and function, its original religious function of bringing people together in a community ceremony where the actors are in some sense priests or celebrants, and the audience is drawn to participate with the actors in a kind of eucharist.

Where this is the admitted function of theater the playwright's work is not so much to "write a play" as to "construct a ceremony" which can be used by the actors to come together with their audience. Words are a part of this ceremony, but not necessarily the dominant part, as they are not the dominant part either in a formal religious ceremony. The important thing is what is happening between the audience and the action. At each point in constructing the ceremony the playwright must say to himself: "What is the audience experiencing now? At what point are they on their journey and where are they to be brought to next?" The "trip" for the audience must be as carefully structured as any ancient mystery or initiation. But the form must reflect contemporary thought processes. And we don't think much in a linear fashion. Ideas overlap, themes recur, archetypal figures and events transform from shape to shape as they dominate our minds.

The creation of this piece was an exploration of certain ideas and images that seem to dominate our minds and lives. The only criterion, finally, of whether or not to follow an impulse in the piece was: Did it work for us or not, in our lives, in our thoughts, and in the playing on the stage.

A large part in the creation of the ceremony was "letting go." For my part, I let go a great many words, characters and scenes. And most painfully I let go certain rigid structural concepts I had invented to replace the linear ones of a conventional play. But whatever was good of these—a funeral, a Catholic mass, an LSD trip, an inquisition, a modern mystery play—remains within the structure of the present ceremony. And so too, lengthy discussions, improvisations, and even unstated common feelings within the company remain somewhere within the final piece—in fact more, probably, than even we can remember.

When other acting groups want to perform *The Serpent* I hope that they will use the words and movements only as a skeleton on which they will put their own flesh. Because *The Serpent* is a ceremony reflecting the minds and lives of the people performing it. What I would like to think is that we have gone deep enough into ourselves to find and express some notions, some images, some feelings which will bring the actors together with the audience, and that these images, these ideas, these feelings, will be found to be held in common.

Jean-Claude van Itallie

FROM THE DIRECTOR

All entertainment is instructive. It instructs the sensibility. It needn't give information in order to instruct. In fact, information can more easily be rejected than the ambiance of the entertainment.

Within the theater it is often believed that except for the concerns of the particular character he is playing, the less an actor knows about the implications of a work, the better. In a work like *The Serpent* the actor must understand as much as can be understood. Here the ideas in the piece are as important to the actor's understanding as are his individual character motivations. Since the strength of the production rests on the power of the ensemble of actors, the ensemble must address itself to the questions and images which make up *The Serpent*. The most hazardous and rewarding problem in a group effort such as this one is to find communal points of reference.

* * *

Because the main part of the piece is taken from a narrative, the story of Genesis in the Bible, it is important that the group of actors first look for images which come close to their own early pictures of these stories. The more faithful their images are to their own garden-in-the-mind, to Adam and Eve, etc., the more Jean-Claude van Itallie's text will emerge. *The text follows the narrative of Genesis, and is at the same time a repudiation of its assumptions, thus forming a dialectic.* What is deeply engaging in the biblical mythology is the discovery that its assumptions are even now the hidden bases of a lot of our making of choices.

The text gives a structure for the playing out of the story, and includes places for the company to improvise. Performing an improvisation is seldom successful without a framework to contain the kinetic happening —that which is going on in the room in a non-verbal, non-literal way. The springboard of the improvisation is within the narrative, such as in the ecstasy of Adam and Eve after the apple has been bitten. But once the actors are in the house playing out the exploration of the ecstasy, there is the other reality of people-players and audience—and here is where the delicate and mysterious encounter takes place. That encounter is not "made," but "permitted." It is not performed at that moment, but let be. It is caused neither by the actor nor by the audience, but by the silence between them.

The actors consciously confront the full bewilderment of people together in a room. Some of the audience are pleased at the shift of focus from the stage to the whole room as a larger stage. Some of the audience have been disgusted with the whole proceedings from the start, and here may express it. And others in the audience are also aware of their own bewilderment. Within the narrative are guideposts which are springboards for the actors to give form to this otherwise formless encounter. The aim in the improvised parts is not simply to assess the players' or the audience's attitudes. The confrontation is with that delicate but powerful pulse of people assembled in the same room. For this reason it is the rhythm and dynamic responses, rather than the confrontation of attitudes between the actor and the audience, which are important. This special task is possible in the particular context of the *anonymous intimacy* between players and audience, and through it the main theme which is the confrontation of our mortality.

* * *

The role of the four women who make up the chorus is multiple. They are, to the audience, hostesses. They are narrator and chorus. They are contemporary widows mourning "the good life." They introduce ideas which are thematic perspectives. They bring everything into question by juxtaposing the worldly with the otherworldly. They "de-mystify" by making common, and yet untenable, statements. They answer questions implied in the rest of the text by further questions, continually intruding on answers to bring into focus the unanswerable.

It would be difficult to overstress the importance of the group effort. In usual theater situations the text is there, and the director follows out his own plan. But in *The Serpent* the text invites all those working on it to create what will happen on stage. The director is the agent through whom the work finds its final plan, but he does not fix anything in his mind before the work begins. The actors collaborate fully, introducing images and possibilities, some of which they will themselves eventually embody on the stage. The collaboration requires that each person address to himself the major questions posited in the material: what are my own early pictures of Adam and Eve and the serpent, of the Garden of Eden, of Cain and Abel? These questions deal with a personal remembered "first time." They are the questions we stopped asking after childhood. We stopped asking them because they were unanswerable (even though we gave or guessed at answers), and later we substituted "adult" answerable questions for them. The group must also go into these deeply dramatic questions of the "first man," "first woman," "first discovery of sex," and also into the character of God in the Old Testament. I would state that the premise of the piece is that Man made God in his own image, and held up this God to determine his own, Man's, limits.

When these questions are alive to the company of actors, there is in

9

any of them a dangerous point when discussion must stop and the questions must be brought to the stage in terms of improvisatory actions. There are two main values in working on a piece in this way, collaboratively. One is the affirming discovery of finding deep common references. It takes time to reach these; the cliché references all need to come out first. And the second value is the astonishing power there is in the performance of an actor who is actually playing out an image which he himself introduced.

* * *

The first steps of collaborative work, then, are to open up and develop a vocabulary of image and action. Later the director becomes more important. He must find ways to select the most cogent from among possible images; he must enlarge any particular image through more specific demands of voice and movement; he must redefine the actors' intentions when they become lost; and he must discover ways to sustain the freshness of successive performances. That part of the work which is a combination of both fixed and improvised-for-the-night must be set up with a carefully thought-out balance, so as to make possible its existence anew each time in the particular room in which it is played. Also, the single action which has been finally chosen for each part of each scene must be a formal articulation of the one choice selected from among many, the one phrase-of-action which represents the essential impulse of the scene.

Why is *The Serpent* a ceremony? What kind of ceremony is it? It is one in which the actors and audience confront the question: where are we at in relation to where we've been? The four women of the chorus go back again and again to references about "the beginning" and "the middle." Anything may have been possible in the beginning, but now we've made the choice, and that choice excludes other possibilities. It makes those choices which are still possible fewer. The ceremony celebrates this point in time: now. We can't remake the past. *The Serpent* insists on our responsibility of acknowledging that we have already gone in a particular direction. It says: where are we at? What are the boundaries we adhere to, and how have they become fixed?

In *The Serpent* the point of crossing a boundary, such as when Eve eats the apple, is a point of transformation, and the whole company crosses a boundary. Because when even one person crosses a forbidden line, nothing is the same for anyone after that.

Joseph Chaikin

A LETTER

Since it was first performed by the Open Theater a couple of years ago I have had the chance to see *The Serpent* performed by three other groups. A couple of these productions were good. One I thought was abysmal. All three tried to make the piece their own, to make the images in it personal to themselves. Also all of them worked on the piece for at least six weeks together, as a company, which I think is the minimum necessary time to spend on it.

I would like to quote a few paragraphs from the angry letter I wrote to the director of the company whose production I so disliked, in the hopes that these will provide some indication to a new director approaching the piece of how I feel it should *not* be done.

* * *

Actors are not poets, at least not while they're on their feet in front of an audience. Their concentration had better not be on the invention of words while they are performing. If it is then the words are at very best, trite, and the performances suffer. There are certain precise and taxing techniques necessary to acting a play like *The Serpent*. The actor needs to be keenly aware and open to himself, to other members of the ensemble, and to the audience—inventing words à la Second City of ten years ago has nothing to do with these techniques at all, and only distracts and detracts from the piece.

What of "improvisation" you say. Aren't ensemble companies supposed to improvise? The word "improvisation" is an overused one and means a lot of different things to different people. What it does *not* mean for a play like *The Serpent* is verbal improvisation in performance . . .

Which moments of freedom within the text the actor does have you can best find in Joseph Chaikin's "director's notes." Just about the only moment of total freedom to follow *any* impulse of the moment comes in the "apple eating," but even here there are restrictions—there has to be a time limit, a ban on the spoken word, and an agreed-upon intent by the company before hand. Otherwise you will lose your audience in terms of the tension of the piece.

I have found that improvisation (and mostly non-verbal at that) works best in inverse proportion to the amount of time left in a rehearsal period before performance. Of course the beginning of rehearsals by the ensemble should be exercises toward the material, and an opening of the actors to it, a personalization—but performance itself must be tight, i.e. the logic of the play, its thrust, has to be clear. This involves an awareness on the part of the director as to how he is using

11

duration, time, and he must above all be economical and even sparing, in order to completely attract the audience's attention and tension where he wants it.

It is necessary that *The Serpent* be tightly performed, because it is such an abstract piece; it attempts to break some kind of barriers in theatrical form, and if you want to be innovative you have a particular responsibility to be *clear* . . .

The two ensemble companies that I know and most respect—The Polish Lab and the Open Theater—never "improvise" during a performance of a play (except in the sense that every good actor and every good company is always improvising). In fact contrary to what is sometimes believed about them by some who haven't seen them, the success of their performances is due in large part to an extreme discipline, albeit one of their own devising.

Finally, another word about the text. . . . Words, as you're aware, have become terribly misused, in life also—we use them to lie and to put up barriers rather than bridges. Contemporaneously a long speech is suspect because speeches are the vehicle by which politicians and other power people deliver us their hypocrisy. "General conversation" most often conforms to the modes and intent of a repressive middle-class atmosphere, and often words curdle in our mouths as we speak them— words feel like traps set by the societal powers that be, physical and metaphysical, and often like a betrayal of where you sense the reality is actually at. To simply transfer such words onto the stage (even to mock them) is very unsatisfactory to me.

What the Open Theater and I tried to do in creating *The Serpent* was to find theatrical expression (nonverbal) of certain questions. In *The Serpent* these questions have to do with guilt and disquiet . . . The process, from the first workshop to the first definitive performance, took a year and some months . . . The words are intended to be few and clear, as poetry—they attempt to be the "top of the iceberg" to the rest of the theatrical experience for the audience, capping off images that have already been sensed . . .

There is, I admit, a trap in the subtitle (A Ceremony). I didn't intend it to be a trap. I used the word "ceremony" to try to break the audience's usual notion of what a play is. But for a company coming to the text in order to perform it, even *as* a ceremony, it is a play in the very usual sense that if you vary the text you do so at your own peril . . . and mine apparently . . .

> Sincerely,
> Jean-Claude van Itallie
> February 20, 1970
> Los Angeles, California

12

The Serpent

In all parts of the theater, including the aisle, the stage and the balcony, the actors warm up. Each does what physical exercises best prepare him for playing. The lights dim slowly and not completely. Each actor wears a costume that seems natural on him particularly, of colorful and easily falling materials that flatter the movement of his body. The total effect, when the company moves together, is kaleidoscopic. The actress who will play Eve wears a simply cut short white dress, and Adam old khaki pants and a shirt with no collar. None of the others is costumed for a particular role. As no one wears any shoes but tights or ballet slippers, a dropcloth for the stage is desirable.

After a few minutes the actors begin to move around the theater in a procession led by an actor who taps out a simple marching rhythm on a bongo drum. The players don't use their voices, but they explore every other sound that can be made by the human body—slapping oneself, pounding one's chest, etc. The actors also use simple and primitive musical instruments during the procession. During some later scenes an actor may accompany the stage action with the repeated sound of a single note on one of these instruments. The procession appears to be one of medieval mummers, and sounds like skeletons on the move. All at once all stop in a freeze. This happens three times during the procession. During a freeze each actor portrays one of various possible motifs from the play such as: the sheep, the serpent, the president's wife's reaching gesture, Adam's movement, Cain's waiting movement, Eve's movement, the heron, and the old people. In countries outside the United States where it is thought that not everyone will immediately recognize all events in the piece, at these motif moments actors shout out the names King and Kennedy.

Transitions from a scene to the next will be done rhythmically, in the character of one scene or of the following, as a slow transformation or "dissolve," or completely out of character with the audience merely watching the actor go to his next place. Each transition is slightly different, but pre-determined.

THE DOCTOR

When the procession is nearly over, the doctor detaches himself from it. A victim, a woman, from among the actors is carried over by two actors and placed on a table formed by three other actors. The doctor stands behind the table. He speaks in a kind of chant. His movements are slow and ritualistic. The rest of the actors, watching, will provide stylized sounds for the operation. A gunshot will be heard once in a while. We will already have heard the gunshot a couple of times during the end of the procession.

DOCTOR

Autopsy:
With a single stroke of the cleaver
The corpse is split open.

Actors make cutting sound from the backs of their throats

The fatty tissues
Fall away
In two yellow folds.

DOCTOR

In a corpse
The blood is black
And does not flow.
In a living person
The blood is black
And flows
From the liver
To the spine, and from
There to the heart
And the brain.
To penetrate the skull
We shave the head,
And cut out a disk of flesh
The shape of a half moon.

Actors make the sound of the saw

We inject the exposed bone
With a steel needle

And push air into the skull
To look into the brain.
Then with a diamond drill
We enter the bone.

Actors make the sound of teeth nibbling

And nibble at the opening
With a hammer, chisel and knife.
The brain is cream-colored.
It is a balance of chemicals.
Thought is effected
By traveling electrons.

Gunshot

During a brain operation
Pressing at this point
With a knife
Causes live patients
To exclaim at sudden memories.
If we press here
We get fear.

Gunshot

The patient, who so far has been lying fairly still, climbs off the
table and comes slowly toward the audience in a state of extreme
bodily tension, making a soundless appeal.

In gunshot wounds
Infection ensues
Unless an operation
Is undertaken immediately.
We excise the wound,
And suck out bits of bone
And diffluent brain matter.
If the patient survives
He may live for weeks
Or months
Or years.

The four women of the chorus make the same small long scream at

17

the backs of their throats that they will make when we later see
Abel's ghost.

He functions barely.
He is unconscious.
Or semi-conscious.
We don't know.
We clean him,
And feed him.
But there is no measure
To what degree
The mind imagines, receives, or dreams.

KENNEDY-KING ASSASSINATION

A cheering crowd forms in a semi-circle at the back of the stage.
Using four chairs, or sitting on the floor if the stage is raked
enough, four actors, two men and two women, sit in the car as the
central characters in the assassination of President John F. Kennedy. The governor and his wife are in front. The President and his
wife are in the back seat exactly as in all the newspaper pictures.
They are waving. The crowd, moving fron one side of the stage to
the other behind them, gives the same impression of movement as
in a film when the scenery is moved behind what is supposed to be
a "moving" car. When the crowd moves the first time, one figure
is left to the side: the assassin. Another figure stands behind the
crowd, and does not move with it. Again, everyone but the people
in the car is facing the audience. The people in the car look at the
audience, smile at them as if they were the crowd. The events
which are the actual assassination are broken down into a count
of twelve, as if seen on a slowed-down silent film. Within this
count all the things which we are told factually happened, happen:

1: All four wave.
2: President is shot in the neck.
3: Governor is shot in the shoulder.
4: President is shot in the head. Governor's wife pulls her husband down and covers him with her body.
5: President falls against his wife.

6: President's wife begins to register something is wrong. She looks at her husband.
7: She puts her hands on his head.
8: She lifts her knee to put his head on it.
9: She looks into the front seat.
10: She begins to realize horror.
11: She starts to get up.
12: She begins to crawl out the back of the open car, and to reach out her hand.

Immediately after that, the numbers are started again. The numbers have been actually shouted aloud by guards who come down toward the front of the stage and kneel, their backs to the audience. Then the count is made a third time, backward this time. The crowd reactions are also backward, as if a film of these events were being run backward. Then the guards call out numbers from one to twelve at random, and the people in the crowd, as well as the characters in the car, assume the positions they had at the time of the particular number being called. The blank-faced assassin has simply mimed shooting a rifle at the count of two. He faces the audience, too. The action in the car continues, as if the count from one to twelve were going on perpetually, but we no longer hear the guards shouting. The crowd, aside from the assassin, forms a tight group at the rear of the right side of the stage. They face the audience. The four women of the chorus are in the front. The crowd shouts and marches very slowly toward the front.
At first, however, we have not understood what they are shouting. The shout is broken down into first vowels, second vowels, center consonants and end consonants. Each of four sections of the crowd has been assigned one part. The shout is repeated four times, each time through adding one of the four parts.

CROWD SHOUT

I was not involved.
I am a small person.
I hold no opinion.
I stay alive.

Then everyone on stage freezes, and the figure at the back quietly speaks words like the actual ones of Dr. Martin Luther King:

19

Though we stand in life at midnight,
I have a dream.
He's allowed me
To go to the mountaintop,
And I've looked over.
I've seen the promised land.
I have a dream
That we are, as always,
On the threshold of a new dawn,
And that we shall all see it together.

The crowd continues its shout, building up the other stanzas as it did the previous one, but the words are still not completely clear. The characters in the car continue their slow-motion actions.

CROWD SHOUT

I mind my own affairs.
I am a little man.
I lead a private life.
I stay alive.

I'm no assassin.
I'm no president.
I don't know who did the killing.
I stay alive.

I keep out of big affairs.
I am not a violent man.
I am very sorry, still
I stay alive.

At times we have been able to make out the words of the President's wife which she has been speaking on count twelve as she reaches out.

PRESIDENT'S WIFE

I've got his brains in my—

The last time through the whole shout, we hear each section of the crowd emphasizing its own part, while the assassin, who has been standing on one side, facing the audience and going through, silently, the agonies of having been himself shot, speaks the words with the others, clearly.

I was not involved.
I am a small person.
I hold no opinions.
I stay alive.

I mind my own affairs.
I am a little man.
I lead a private life.
I stay alive.

I'm no assassin.
I'm no president.
I don't know who did the killing.
I stay alive.

I keep out of big affairs.
I am not a violent man.
I am very sorry, still
I stay alive.

THE GARDEN

Everyone's breath comes short and heavy and rhythmically, as if in surprise. The four chorus women dressed in black detach themselves from the rest of the group and in short spurts of movement and speech go to the downstage right area, facing the audience.

FIRST WOMAN OF THE CHORUS
I no longer live in the beginning.

SECOND WOMAN OF THE CHORUS
I've lost the beginning.

THIRD WOMAN OF THE CHORUS
I'm in the middle,
Knowing.

THIRD AND FOURTH WOMEN OF THE CHORUS

Neither the end
Nor the beginning.

FIRST WOMAN

I'm in the middle.

SECOND WOMAN

Coming from the beginning.

THIRD AND FOURTH WOMEN

And going toward the end.

In the meantime, others are forming the creatures in the garden of Eden. They, too, emanate from the same communal "first breath." Many of the creatures are personal, previously selected by each actor as expressing an otherwise inexpressible part of himself. For the audience, perhaps the heron has the most identifiable reality. He moves about gently, tall, proud, in slow spurts; he stands on one foot, moves his wings slightly, occasionally, and makes a soft "brrring" noise. Other creatures become distinguishable. The serpent is formed by five (male) actors all writhing together in a group, their arms, legs, hands, tongues, all moving.

The chorus women have repeated their "in the beginning" lines from above. They speak these lines as a secret to the audience.

* * *

There is a sense of awe about the whole creation of the garden. The two human creatures also become discernible. As Eve sits up and sees the world, she screams in amazement. The sound of her scream is actually made by one of the four chorus women. They are also Eve. They think of themselves as one person, and any one of them at this moment might reflect Eve.

Adam falls asleep. The heron and the serpent are now more clearly discernible from the other creatures. The creatures play with themselves and each other quietly, in awe. The serpent is feeling out the environment with hands and mouths and fingers. There is nothing orgiastic about the garden—on the contrary, there is the restraint of curious animals in a strange environment.

22

SERPENT 1: Is it true?
SERPENT 2: Is it true
SERPENT 3: That you and he,
SERPENT 4: You and he
SERPENT 4 and 5: May do anything?
SERPENT 2: Anything in the garden you want to do?
SERPENT 1: Is that true?

EVE: We may do anything
Except one thing.

FIRST WOMAN OF THE CHORUS:
We may do anything
Except one thing.

In the dialogue between Eve and the serpent the first of the chorus
women echoes Eve's lines, but with the emphasis placed on different words. The four chorus women look at the audience as if it
were the serpent in front of them. The serpent speaks and hisses
to Eve with all his five mouths. Care must be taken by the actors
playing the serpent that all the words are heard distinctly, despite
overlap in speaking. Eve is almost in a state of tremor at being
alive. The serpent is seducing her with his even greater aliveness,
as well as with the intellectual argument. As Eve comes closer to
being in the state the serpent is in, her movements begin to imitate
the serpent's, and she, finally, is seducing him, too. Some of the
other actors are now seated on a bench facing the audience, at
the back of the stage where they sit, and rest, and pay attention to
the action. This is where those who are not playing a particular
scene will always go—none of the actors will ever actually leave
the stage. During Eve's dialogue with the serpent, only the heron
and one or two other animals in the garden are upright, but they
do not distract our attention. The serpent is not only the serpent,
he is also the tree, and he holds apples.

SERPENT 2: What one thing?
EVE: We are not allowed to eat from the tree.
FIRST WOMAN: We are not allowed
To eat from the tree.
SERPENT 3: Not allowed to eat?

EVE: We may not even touch it.
WOMAN: We may not even touch it.

SERPENT 1: Not even touch?
SERPENT 4 and 5: Not touch?
SERPENT 5: Why not even touch?

EVE: Adam said I would die.
WOMAN: Adam said I would die.

The serpent is gently surrounding her until she has touched him without her realizing it.

SERPENT 3: If you—
SERPENT 4: If you touch—
SERPENT 4 and 5: If you touch the tree—
SERPENT 1: Adam said
SERPENT 2: If you touch the tree
SERPENT 4 and 5: If you even touch the tree
You will die—
SERPENT 1: But—
SERPENT 2: But—
SERPENT 3: But—

Eve realizes her back is against the tree.

SERPENT 5: Have you died?
SERPENT 4 (*Whispering*): Have you died?

EVE: I don't know.
WOMAN: I don't know.

SERPENT 2: You touched the tree.
SERPENT 2 and 3: And you haven't died.
SERPENT 4: You haven't died.

EVE: But Adam said—
WOMAN: But Adam said—

SERPENT 1: Oh, Adam said
SERPENT 2: Adam said, Adam said . . .

SERPENT 1 and 2: Listen.
SERPENT 2 and 3: Answer me this.
SERPENT 5 (*overlapping the others*): This.

SERPENT 4: Could it?
SERPENT 3: Could it hurt more
To eat than to touch?
SERPENT 5: To eat than to touch?
SERPENT 1: Could it?

EVE: It is forbidden.
WOMAN: It is forbidden.

SERPENT 2: Who has forbidden it?
SERPENT 1: Who?

EVE: God.
WOMAN: God.

SERPENT 4: And why?
SERPENT 5: Why has he forbidden it?
SERPENT 4: Why?
SERPENT 3: Why does he set limits
SERPENT 2 and 3: Against you and Adam?
SERPENT 1: Think.
SERPENT 2: Is the fruit God's property?
SERPENT 3: Is it?
SERPENT 1: He says Adam and Eve may not eat.
But are Adam and Eve
Guests in this garden?
SERPENT 2: Are they guests?
SERPENT 1: Don't they live here?
SERPENT 3: May they not eat where they want?

EVE: (*Turning away*): I don't know.
WOMAN: I don't know.

SERPENT 5: Also, also haven't you
SERPENT 4 and 5: Haven't you noticed
SERPENT 4: That the younger always have rule
Over the elder creation?
SERPENT 2: Haven't you noticed,
and aren't you afraid?
SERPENT 1: Aren't you afraid
And hadn't you better hurry
SERPENT 1 and 2: And eat the fruit now

Before the next comes to rule
Over you?

EVE: I'm not afraid.
WOMAN: I'm not afraid.

SERPENT (to itselves) 1: She's not afraid.
SERPENT 2: Why should she be?
SERPENT 3: How could she be?
SERPENT 4: How?
SERPENT 5: She couldn't be,
She doesn't know.
SERPENT 4: Doesn't know what?
SERPENT 3: Doesn't know she exists.
SERPENT 4: Why doesn't she know it?
SERPENT 3: Because she hasn't eaten.
SERPENT 2: If she'd eaten, she'd know.
SERPENT 1: Know what?
SERPENT 4: What worlds she would know
If she ate.
SERPENT 5: What worlds?
SERPENT 1: If she ate she would know
SERPENT 1 and 2: And if she knew
SERPENT 1 AND 2 AND 3: She could—

EVE: What?
WOMAN: What?

SERPENT 4: You don't know
SERPENT 5: Because you haven't eaten.

EVE: Do you know?
WOMAN: Do you know?

SERPENT 2: I don't know.
SERPENT 1: I don't.
SERPENT 3: But I can imagine.
SERPENT 4: Imagine.
SERPENT 5: Imagine.

EVE: But, is what you can imagine
What will be?

26

WOMAN: But, is what you can imagine
What will be?

SERPENT 1 AND 2: How can you know
Until you eat?
SERPENT 5: How can I know?
SERPENT 4: How can I know until you eat?
SERPENT 1: This garden
SERPENT 2: All these animals and these plants
SERPENT 2 AND 3: Were once only imagined.

EVE: Shall I risk losing all these?
WOMAN: Shall I risk losing all these?

SERPENT 1: It may be.
SERPENT 2: It may be that no garden
SERPENT 4: Is better than this one.
SERPENT 5: This garden.
SERPENT 4: It may be.
SERPENT 2: But you won't know,
SERPENT 1: You can't know
Until you eat.
SERPENT 2: How could you know?

EVE: If I eat
And if I die
Will you die too?
WOMAN: If I eat
And if I die
Will you die too?

SERPENT 1: If you die
I will die too.

EVE: Why do you want me to eat?
WOMAN: Why do you want me to eat?

SERPENT 5: Because I want
SERPENT 4: I want to
SERPENT 3: I want to know.

EVE: Know what?
WOMAN: Know what?

27

SERPENT 2: Know what you will know.
SERPENT 1: Know what will happen.

EVE: I might.
I might do it.
I might do it if God didn't know.
WOMAN: I might.
I might do it.
I might do it if God didn't know.

SERPENT 3: You might
SERPENT 4: Might do it if God didn't know?
SERPENT 2: But you want to.
SERPENT 1: And he knows you want to.
SERPENT 5: Is a crime
SERPENT 4: Only a crime
SERPENT 5: When you're caught?

EVE: Shall I do what I want to then?
WOMAN: Shall I do what I want to then?

SERPENT 1 AND 2 AND 3 AND 4 AND 5: Yes!

EVE: Even if what I want is to listen
To God and not to you?
WOMAN: Even if what I want is to listen
To God and not to you?

SERPENT 1: Yes.
SERPENT 2: If you want.
SERPENT 3 AND 4: If you want.
SERPENT 5: Yes.

EVE: Then I will eat.
WOMAN: Then I will eat.

She bites into one of the apples held by the many hands of the
serpent.

EVE: Because I want to.
WOMAN: Because I want to.

EATING THE APPLE

When Eve finally eats she is seated in the middle of the serpent. After a couple of frantic bites, there is a pause as Eve begins to savor the experience. The first woman of the chorus, who echoed Eve's words to the serpent, now describes Eve's experience.

FIRST WOMAN OF THE CHORUS

And Eve looked
At the creatures in the garden,
And at the ground
And at the wind and the water,
And she said: I am not the same as these.
And she began to examine
Her skin and her eyes
And her ears and her nose and her mouth.
And she began to examine her own mind.
And Eve went to Adam
To persuade him to eat.
But Adam said:
"You have eaten of that which was forbidden, and you shall die.
Do you want me to eat and die too?"

Eve in a kind of frenzy has gone over to Adam, woken him up, and is trying to have him eat. He, at first, refuses but then is caught up in her frenzy and he eats too. After his first bite nothing seems to happen. The serpent freezes during Adam and Eve's argument but he has shared Eve's ecstasy. The three other women of the chorus "davenn" while the first woman describes the action. This davenning is a rhythmic murmur like that of old women in churches and synagogues as they repeat and repeat familiar prayers and laments.

FIRST WOMAN OF THE CHORUS

But Adam ate.
And Adam looked
At the creatures in the garden,
And at the ground
And at the wind and the water,
And he said: I am not the same as these.
And he began to examine
His skin and his eyes

29

And his ears and his nose and his mouth.
And he began to examine his own mind.
And he could neither spit out the fruit
Nor could he swallow it.

Adam takes a second bite. All the actors, in a kind of ecstasy, form the serpent, moving in the same manner as we saw the serpent move with fewer actors earlier. The serpent, as played by all the actors, is still a display of the tree of life. It is seductive and inviting. Then the serpent separates.

A bag of apples is found on one side of the stage. An actor empties it out on the stage. The actors play with the apples, eat them, and carry them out to the audience to share their pleasure with them.

THE CURSES

Adam begins to cough a little. It is clear that he can indeed neither swallow the fruit nor spit it out. Suddenly, an actor who has been playing one of the creatures in the garden pulls Adam up from under the arms. Adam himself speaks for God when God is speaking to Adam. When speaking for God, Adam uses a voice which is larger and more resonant than his usual one, and the actor who lifts him mouths the same words. Adam's own attitude, as he speaks for God, is one of surprise and dismay. Whenever God will speak, all the actors on stage will whisper his words too.

GOD (*speaking through Adam*)
Where are you?

The actor who had lifted Adam up now drops him and goes back to playing a creature in the garden. Adam tries to hide, and he tries to cough up the fruit to be able to speak clearly to God. But the fruit remains stuck in his throat. The same actor picks him up again.

GOD (*speaking through Adam*)
Where are you?
Why do you not answer me?

The actor lets Adam drop and becomes a creature in the garden again.

30

ADAM (*answering God*)

I hear your voice in the garden
And I am afraid.

Adam is picked up again. Whenever he is picked up to speak, his
body goes limp.

GOD (*speaking through Adam*)

Before
When you heard my voice
You were not afraid,
Yet, now you are afraid.

Adam is dropped again.

ADAM (*answering God*)

I am afraid
Because I am naked
And I have hidden myself.

Adam is picked up again from under the arms.

GOD (*speaking through Adam*)

Who told you
You were naked?
Have you eaten of the tree
From which
I commanded you not to eat?

Adam is dropped.

ADAM (*answering*)

Lord, so long as I was alone
I did not fall into sin.
But as soon as this woman came
She tempted me.

Another actor now lifts up Eve in the same way Adam was lifted,
and Eve is limp and speaks for God in a voice that is larger and
more resonant than her usual one. The actor who lifts her, and the
others, whisper the same words she is speaking.

GOD (*speaking through Eve*)

Woman, have you eaten of the tree
Whereof I commanded you not to eat?

Eve is let drop, and the actor who had lifted her goes back to playing a creature in the garden.

EVE (*answering God*)

It was the serpent, Lord.
He tempted me, and I ate.

SERPENT 1: You gave them a command,
and I contradicted it.
SERPENT 2: Why did they obey me
And not you?

From now on the voice of God is heard similarly through the different actors on the stage. All, except the four women of the chorus, lift each other in turn and speak with a voice that is larger than their usual ones. After lifting or being lifted, the actors return to being creatures in the garden. As the curses continue, there is a shorter space of time between them, and greater agitation in the garden. And as the curses are spoken each by one actor, the other actors simultaneously whisper them to the audience.

GOD (*speaking through one actor who is lifted from under his arms by another actor*)

Because you have done this
You are cursed over all animals.
Upon your belly shall you go
And dust shall you eat.

GOD (*speaking through another actor*)

Because you have eaten
Of the tree of which I commanded you,
Saying: You shall not eat of it,
Cursed is the earth for your sake.

GOD (*speaking through another actor*)

You shall use your mind
Not to understand but to doubt.
And even if you understand,
Still shall you doubt.

GOD (*speaking through another actor*)

When your children shall be found to murder,

32

You shall make laws.
But these laws shall not bind.

GOD (*speaking through another actor*)
You shall be made to think,
And although few of your thoughts shall exalt you,
Many of your thoughts shall bring you sorrow,
And cause you to forget your exaltation.

GOD (*speaking through another actor*)
Now shall come a separation
Between the dreams inside your head
And those things which you believe
To be outside your head
And the two shall war within you.

GOD (*speaking through another actor*)
Accursed, you shall be alone.
For whatever you think,
And whatever you see or hear,
You shall think it and see it and hear it, alone.
Henceforth shall you thirst after me.

GOD (*speaking through another actor*)
In the day shall you endure
The same longing as in the night,
And in the night shall you endure
The same longing as in the day.
Henceforth shall you thirst after me.

GOD (*speaking through another actor*)
And your children shall live in fear of me.
And your children shall live in fear of you,
And your children shall live in fear of each other.

GOD (*speaking through another actor*)
Accursed, you shall glimpse Eden
All the days of your life.
But you shall not come again.
And if you should come,
You would not know it.

33

GOD (*speaking through another actor*)

And in the end
The earth shall wax old like a garment
And be cast off by me.

GOD (*speaking through another actor*)

For that you were not able to observe the command
Laid upon you, for more than one hour,
Accursed be your days.
Henceforth shall you thirst after me.

* * *

With the volume increasing, the curses begin to overlap. They
are repeated and fragmented, spoken and whispered louder by an
increasing number of actors. Many actors are regularly picked up
and dropped. It becomes increasingly impossible to distinguish
whole phrases. All the voices build into a frenzy and a din of
sound.

And in the day
Shall you endure the same longing
As in the night.

Henceforth shall you thirst after me.

And in the night
Shall you endure the same longing
As in the day.

Henceforth shall you thirst after me.

And now shall come a separation.

Accursed.

Between the dreams inside your head.

Accursed.

And those things which you believe to be outside your head
And the two shall war within you.

And your children shall live in fear of me.

And in the end the earth shall wax old like a garment

34

And be cast off by me.

And your children shall live in fear of you.

You shall not come again to Eden.

And your children shall live in fear of each other.

And if you should come, you would not know it.

Accursed, you shall be made to think.

Accursed, you shall be alone.

And even when you understand,
Still shall you doubt.

Accursed.

Accursed.

Accursed.

Suddenly, there is silence. All the actors remain frozen a few
seconds. Then Adam and Eve repeat, and continue to repeat
throughout the next scene, their "locked" action of, respectively,
accusing, and of reaching and subsiding.

STATEMENTS I

The four women are still kneeling.

FIRST WOMAN OF THE CHORUS
In the beginning anything is possible.

SECOND WOMAN OF THE CHORUS
I've lost the beginning.

THIRD WOMAN OF THE CHORUS
I'm in the middle.

FOURTH WOMAN OF THE CHORUS
Knowing neither the end nor the beginning.

Now they stand. They sway slightly from side to side.

FIRST WOMAN
One lemming.

One lemming.

One lemming.

One lemming.

When they are not speaking their own statements each of the women continues to say softly "one lemming" as an accompaniment to what the others are saying.

FIRST WOMAN

I try sometimes to imagine what it's like to be somebody else.
But it's always me pretending.
It has to be me.
Who else is there?

SECOND WOMAN

I hugged my child
And sent him off to school
With his lunch in a paper bag.
And I wished he would never come home.

THIRD WOMAN

I'm concerned
Because what you reject
Can still run your life.

FOURTH WOMAN

I passed my friend on the street.

SECOND WOMAN

I passed quite near.

FOURTH WOMAN

I don't think she saw me.
If she did, I don't think

SECOND WOMAN

She saw me see her.

FOURTH WOMAN

I think she thought

36

SECOND WOMAN

If she saw me

FOURTH WOMAN

That I didn't see her.

THIRD WOMAN

If God exists
It is through me.
And He will protect me
Because He owes His existence to me.

FIRST WOMAN

Old stories
Have a secret.

SECOND WOMAN

They are a prison.

THIRD WOMAN

Someone is locked inside them.

FOURTH WOMAN

Sometimes, when it's very quiet,
I can hear him breathing.

SECOND WOMAN

Sometimes I feel there's nothing to do
But help other people.
But as soon as I join a committee or a party
I know that has nothing to do with it at all.

FOURTH WOMAN

Whatever I know

SECOND WOMAN

I know it without words.

FOURTH WOMAN

I am here as a witness.

SECOND WOMAN

To what?

I don't know.

It was different when I was a child.
I don't see any more bright colors.
There are no solid blocks
Or familiar rooms.

I went to a dinner.
The guests were pleasant.
We were poised,
Smiling over our plates,
Asking and answering the usual questions.
I wanted to throw the food,
Ax the table,
Scratch the women's faces,
And grab the men's balls.

When asked, I blamed it on the other person.
It wasn't me, I said.
It must have been her.
I could have said it was me,
But I said it was her.

My home was Cleveland.
Then I came to New York
And I didn't have to account to anybody.
I smoked: pot, hashish, opium.
I slept with a man.
I slept with a woman.
I slept with a man and a woman at the same time.
But I'm a gentle person, and I collapsed.

I'm still a child.

So am I.

Sometimes people nod at you,
And smile,
And you know they haven't heard.

FIRST WOMAN

On a certain day

SECOND WOMAN

Of a certain year

THIRD WOMAN

One lemming

FOURTH WOMAN

Starts to run.

FIRST WOMAN

Another lemming, seeing the first,

SECOND WOMAN

Drops everything,

THIRD WOMAN

And starts to run too.

FOURTH WOMAN

Little by little

FIRST WOMAN

All the lemmings

SECOND WOMAN

From all over the country

THIRD WOMAN

Run together

FOURTH WOMAN

For tens

FIRST WOMAN

And hundreds of miles

SECOND WOMAN

Until,

FOURTH WOMAN
Exhausted,

FIRST WOMAN

They reach the cliff

SECOND WOMAN

And throw themselves

THIRD WOMAN

Into the sea.

CAIN AND ABEL

The four women continue to davenn, but now without words, except when indicated. Davenning-without-words is like a rhythmic
humming, and it continues under the voices of the individual
women who are speaking. Cain chops wood. Abel tends two sheep.
The scene begins slowly to unfold between them. It will continue
beyond the recital of the action by the chorus.

FOURTH WOMAN

And when they were cast out
Eve and Adam remembered me.
And Eve conceived
And bore Cain,
And she said:

FOURTH AND SECOND WOMEN

"Lo, I have gotten
A man from the Lord."

FOURTH WOMAN

And again Adam and Eve remembered me.
And Eve bore Abel.
And again she said:

FOURTH AND SECOND WOMEN

"Lo, I have gotten
A man from the Lord."

FOURTH WOMAN

Then Eve had a dream,

And she ran and told it to Adam.
And Eve said:
"Lo, I saw Adam's blood flow from Cain's mouth."
And wishing to divert any evil that might come,
Adam separated Cain from Abel.
And Cain became a tiller of the ground,
And Abel a keeper of sheep.
And in time Cain offered unto the Lord
A sacrifice of first fruits,
While his brother Abel offered a firstborn lamb.
And the Lord had love for Abel and for his offering.
But for Cain and for his offering
The Lord had no respect.
And Cain said:

FOURTH AND FIRST WOMEN

"Why did He accept your offering
And not mine?"

FOURTH WOMAN

And Cain's face grew dark,
And his words were not pleasing to the Lord,
And Cain said:

FOURTH AND FIRST WOMEN

"Why did He accept your offering
And not mine?"

FOURTH WOMAN

"There is no law
And there is no judge."
And the Lord spoke within him,
And He said:
"If you will amend your ways
I will forgive your anger.
Yet even now the power of evil
Crouches at the door."
But it occurred to Cain
That the world was created through goodness,
Yet he saw that good deeds bear no fruit.
And God said:
"It depends on you

41

Whether you shall be master over evil,
Or evil over you."
And Cain said:

FOURTH AND FIRST WOMEN

"Why did He accept your offering
And not mine?"

FOURTH WOMAN

And it occurred to Cain
That the world
Is ruled with an arbitrary power.
And Cain said:
"There is no law and there is no judge."

FOURTH AND FIRST WOMEN

"Else
Why did He not accept my offering,
Yet He accepted yours?"

FOURTH WOMAN

And it occurred to Cain
To kill his brother.
But it did not occur to Cain
That killing his brother
Would cause his brother's death.
For Cain did not know how to kill
And he struck at his brother.
And broke each of his bones in turn
And this was the first murder.
And Cain said:
"If I were to spill your blood on the ground
As you do the sheep's,
Who is there to demand it of me?"
And Abel said:
"The Lord will demand it. The Lord will judge."
And Cain said:
"There is no judge. There is no law."

FOURTH AND FIRST WOMEN

"Else
Why did He accept your offering
And not accept mine?"

"Why yours?
Why not mine?"
And it occurred to Cain
To kill his brother.
But it did not occur to Cain
That killing his brother
Would cause his brother's death.
For Cain did not know how to kill.
And he struck at his brother
And broke each of his bones in turn.
And Abel said: "The Lord will judge."
And Cain said:
"There is no judge. There is no law."

FOURTH AND FIRST WOMEN

"Else
Why did he accept your offering
And not accept mine?"

FOURTH WOMAN

"Why yours?
Why not mine?"
And this was the first murder.
For it occurred to Cain
To kill his brother.
But it did not occur to Cain
That killing his brother
Would cause his brother's death.

Cain has come over to Abel. He feeds Abel's sheep, to get them out of his way. He looks at Abel, and Abel looks back at Cain. The rest of the actors, not including the chorus, breathe together regularly and quietly—they are breathing Abel's breath. Cain tries different ways of killing Abel. After trying each different way, he looks at Abel to see the result of what he has done, and to try to decide what to do next. The rest of the company watches, and the sheep remain quietly by. Some of the things that Cain does to Abel are to pull at his limbs, to hold him in the air and think of dashing him on the ground. Finally, he lays Abel down on the ground, and seeing that there is still movement in the respiratory area, Cain uses his hands to chop at Abel's throat. Abel's breathing stops. All the sounds for hurting Abel and for the chopping at him with his hands have come from the actor playing Cain, rather than from the actor playing Abel. Now Cain listens for Abel's breathing, which he misses hearing. He tries to breathe breath back into Abel from his own mouth. Then he tries to stand Abel up. He puts grass into his lifeless hand to try to have Abel feed the sheep. Finally, he lays Abel down on the backs of his two sheep, standing behind him, swaying slightly from side to side, waiting, waiting for life to start up again in Abel. The heron from the garden is back, and it wanders near, making its gentle noise and standing on one leg and then the other. Cain continues to wait. The four women of the chorus make a small, long screeching sound from the backs of their throats. Abel, as a ghost, now crawls on his knees toward the front of the stage. He confronts the audience. The actor playing Abel is, at this moment, experiencing extreme tension throughout his body, and reseeing in his mind's eye what just happened to him. Cain, still watching the place where he put Abel's body on the sheep, continues to wait.

BLIND MEN'S HELL

The two actors who played the sheep, and one other actor, are on their backs on the floor. All the others, with the exception of the chorus, walk around and through them. All are blind and as if experiencing tremendous fatigue. They are like people who have lived too long. None of those who are walking may stop or fall— if they do, they must immediately get up and go on. Those on the floor grope upward, grabbing at parts of the moving people. This continues during Statements II.

STATEMENTS II

FIRST WOMAN OF THE CHORUS

In the beginning
Anything is possible.
From the center
I can choose to go anywhere.

SECOND WOMAN OF THE CHORUS

But now the point
Toward which I have chosen to go
Has a line drawn
Between itself
And the beginning.

FOURTH WOMAN OF THE CHORUS

I no longer know the beginning.
I am in the middle.
On a line
Between the beginning
And a point toward which I chose to go.

THIRD WOMAN OF THE CHORUS

I have fewer choices now.
Because when I change my direction
The change can only start
From a line already drawn.

Now the four women smile. They keep smiling unless they are speaking. They sway slightly from side to side.

SECOND WOMAN

I'm collecting things.
Beads.
I'm buying plants,
Curtains—
With which to make a home.
I'm buying things
To make a good life.

THIRD WOMAN

When I was thirteen
I wanted a house of my own.
The girl I was then
Would say to me now:
"What have you done with your advantages?"
You could have married a rich man,
And had a big house.
Instead, you're a freak."

FIRST WOMAN (*as the other women and herself open and close one fist*)
Open.
Close.
Open.
Close.
No effort
Makes these two movements
One.

SECOND WOMAN
My husband is in that coffin.
In the day he goes to work.
In the evening we discuss household matters,
And at night
He climbs back into the coffin.

THIRD WOMAN
Even if you sit and do nothing,
Even so,
Your back is strapped to a wheel,
And the wheel turns.

FOURTH WOMAN
While we were in bed I asked a boy,

SECOND WOMAN
I asked him if he should be around

FIRST WOMAN
If he should be around when I die,
Would he hold and rock me in his arms
For half an hour afterwards.

THIRD WOMAN
Because they can't tell.

FOURTH WOMAN
They can only approximate.

SECOND WOMAN
They can't tell when you're really dead.

Not exactly.

Not the exact moment.

When I was a child
This story was told to me in secret by a friend:
"A little boy came into his mother's room
And saw her naked.
'What's that?' he asked.
'It's a wound,' she said.
'What happened to your penis?' he asked.
'Oh,' she said,
'God chopped it off with an ax.' "

THIRD WOMAN (*with other women speaking and emphasizing the words "he," "his," and "him"*)
It's my husband.
He keeps me from it.
It's *his* fault.
He keeps me down, holds me at *his* level.
I could be happy
If it weren't for *him*.

The doctors lie.
My mother died screaming with pain.
Did you know you could go into eternity
Screaming with pain?

FIRST WOMAN (*as the other women and herself open and close one fist*)
Open.
Close.
Separate movements.
Stretched-out fingers.
Nails into skin.
One to open.
One to close.
Separate

Motions.
No matter how I try,
These movements
Are not one.
There is a stop between open
And close, and between close
And open.
No effort
Makes these two movements
One.
Close.
Open.
Close.

SECOND WOMAN

You can see them having lunch,

FIRST WOMAN

Their faces pale,

THIRD WOMAN

Laughing.
They are corpses laughing.

FOURTH WOMAN

You can see them on the streets,

SECOND WOMAN

Combed and brushed.

FIRST WOMAN

They are colored pictures.

FIRST AND THIRD WOMEN

The men have killed each other.

SECOND AND FOURTH WOMEN

The king is dead.

FOURTH WOMAN

He was shot in the head.

FIRST WOMAN

By an unknown assassin.

The men are dead.

And no man can say
Of work or land:
"This is mine."

The men are dead.

We mourn them.

We are dead.

We mourn ourselves.

If a bulldog ant
Is cut in two,
A battle starts
Between the head and the tail.
The head bites the tail.
The tail stings the head.
They fight
Until both halves are dead.

So Man created God.
What for?
To set limits on himself.

Would my dreams recognize me?
Would they come to me and say
"She's the one who imagined us"?

I was queen over a country
Where the air was sweet.
We ate honey and fruit.

49

And at night
It was quiet.

Suddenly—
This moment.
Here, now.
I am here,
And you.
In this place, now
We are together.

FIRST WOMAN (*as the other three women, and finally she, begin to make the body sounds of the entering procession*)
At the very end.
Even after the end,
Even when the body is on its own,
The human being can make such a variety
Of sounds that it's amazing.
A field of dead men is loud.
Teeth clack, bones crack,
Limbs twist and drop,
And the last sound of all
Is a loud trumpet
Of escaping wind.

BEGATTING

Now all together the four women begin davenning again, for a moment without words. The Blind Men's Hell has dissolved. Two actors, a man and a woman, begin very slowly approaching each other from either side of the stage. The four women are kneeling and rocking back and forth. All the others begin gently to explore each other's bodies.

THIRD WOMAN (*as the other three davenn under her words*)
And Adam knew Eve and Eve knew Adam
And this was the first time.
And Adam knew Eve and Eve knew Adam
And this was the first time.

The actors are exploring each other's bodies as if for the first time. The women now open a book and read the "begats" from the Old Testament of the Bible. Each woman reads some part and then passes the book to another. But all are continually davenning and, frequently, the exact words of the begatting are lost in favor of the rhythmic davenning and the rocking back and forth toward the audience.

THIRD WOMAN (*reading*)

And Adam lived a hundred and thirty years and he begat a son in his own likeness and he called his name Seth.

And the days of Adam after he had begotten Seth were eight hundred years, and he begat sons and daughters.

And Seth lived a hundred and five years and he begat Enos.

And Seth lived after he begat Enos eight hundred and seven years, and he begat sons and daughters.

And Enos lived ninety years and he begat Cainan.

And Enos lived after he begat Cainan eight hundred and fifteen years, and he begat sons and daughters.

And Cainan lived seventy years and begat Mahalaleel.

The man and woman come closer and closer to touching. The others have paired off, too, and are still exploring bodies.

FOURTH WOMAN (*reading*)

And Cainan lived, after he begat Mahalaleel, eight hundred and forty years, and he begat sons and daughters.

And Mahalaleel lived sixty and five years, and he begat Jared.

And Mahalaleel lived, after he begat Jared, eight hundred and thirty years, and he begat sons and daughters.

And Jared lived a hundred and sixty and two years, and he begat Enoch.

And Jared lived after he begat Enoch eight hundred years, and he begat sons and daughters.

And Enoch lived sixty and five years and he begat Methuselah.

And Enoch walked with God after he begat Methuselah three hundred years, and he begat sons and daughters.

And Enoch walked with God and he was not, for God took him.

And Methuselah lived a hundred and eighty and seven years, and he begat Lamech.

And Methuselah lived after he begat Lamech seven hundred and eighty and two years, and he begat sons and daughters.

And Lamech lived a hundred eighty and two years and he begat a son, and he called his name Noah.

And Lamech lived after he begat Noah five hundred and ninety years, and he begat sons and daughters.

And Noah was five hundred years old, and Noah begat Shem and Ham and Japheth.

By now, the two people have met in the center of the stage and embraced. All the couples are now exploring each other more gymnastically. They are trying to find how to make the connection between the male and the female body. They try various difficult positions. Eventually all make the connection and they copulate in increasingly faster rhythm.

FIRST WOMAN (*reading*)

And these are the generations of the sons of Noah and Shem and Ham and Japheth and the sons that were born to them after the flood:

The sons of Japheth were Gomer and Magog and Madai and Javan and Tubal and Meshech and Tiras.

And the sons of Gomer were Ashkenaz and Riphath and Togarmah.

And the sons of Javan were Elishah and Tarshish and Kittim and Dodanim.

And the sons of Ham were Cush and Mizraim and Phut and Canaan.

And the sons of Cush were Seba and Havilah and Sabtah and Raamah and Sabtechah.

And the sons of Raamah were Sheba and Dedan.

And Cush begat Nimrod, and he began to be a mighty one on earth.

And Canaan begat Sidon, his firstborn, and Heth.

And unto Shem were born Elam and Ashur and Arphaxad and Lud and Aram.

And the children of Aram were Uz and Hul and Gether and Mash.

And Arphaxad begat Salah, and Salah begat Eber.

And unto Eber were born two sons, and one was called Peleg, and his brother's name was Joktan.

And Joktan begat Almodad and Shelaph and Hazarmaveth and Jerah.

And Hadoram and Uzal and Diklah.

All the couples reach their climax at approximately the same time. Immediately afterward, the women go into labor, and they then give birth. Their sons are played by the actors who played their lovers. After the birth, the mothers teach their children how to talk, walk, play games, etc.

SECOND WOMAN (*reading*)

And Obal and Abimael and Sheba,
and Ophir and Havilah and Johab.
All these were the sons of Joktan.
And these were the generations of Shem.
Shem was a hundred years old and begat Arphaxad two years after the flood.

And Shem lived after he begat Arphaxad five hundred years, and he begat sons and daughters.

And Arphaxad lived five and thirty years and he begat Salah.

And Arphaxad lived after he begat Salah four hundred and three years, and he begat sons and daughters.

And Salah lived thirty years and he begat Eber.

And Salah lived after he begat Eber four hundred and three years, and he begat sons and daughters.

And Eber lived four hundred and thirty years and he begat Peleg.

And Eber lived after he begat Peleg four hundred and thirty years, and he begat sons and daughters.

And Peleg lived thirty years and he begat Reu.

And Peleg lived after he begat Reu two hundred and nine years, and he begat sons and daughters.

And Reu lived thirty and two years, and he begat Serug.

And Reu lived after he begat Serug two hundred and seven years, and he begat sons and daughters.

And Serug lived thirty years and he begat Nahor.

And Serug lived after he begat Nahor two hundred years, and he begat sons and daughters.

And Nahor lived twenty and nine years, and he begat Terah.

And Nahor lived after he begat Terah a hundred and nineteen years and he begat sons and daughters.

And Terah lived seventy years, and he begat Abram and Nahor and Haran.

And these are the generations of Terah.

From being small children, the men of the company have become very old people. They are brought forward, helped slowly, to the front of the stage by their mothers, who have remained young. One or two of the actresses play old women and also stay at the front of the stage.

Terah begat Isaac, and Isaac begat Jacob and Jacob begat Judah and his brethren.

And Judah begat Phares and Zarah, of Thamar.

And Phares begat Esrom.

And Esrom begat Aram.

And Aram begat Aminadab.

And Aminadab begat Naasson.

And Naasson begat Salmon.

And Salmon begat Booz, of Rachab.

And Booz begat Obed, of Ruth.

And Obed begat Jesse.

And Jesse begat David the king.

And David the king begat Solomon, of her that had been the wife of Urias.

And Solomon begat Rehoboam.

And Rehoboam begat Abia.

And Abia begat Asa.

And Asa begat Josaphat.

And Josaphat begat Joram.

And Joram begat Ozias.

And Ozias begat Joatham.

And Joatham begat Achaz.

And Achaz begat Ezekias.

And Ezekias begat Manasses.

And Manasses begat Amon.

And Amon begat Josias.

And Josias begat Jechonias and his brethren about the time they were carried away to Babylon.

And after they were brought to Babylon, Jechonias begat Salathiel.

And Salathiel begat Zorobabel.

And Zorobabel begat Abiud.

And Abiud begat Eliakim.
And Eliakim begat Azor.
And Azor begat Sadoc.
And Sadoc begat Achim.
And Achim begat Eliud.
And Eliud begat Eleazur.
And Eleazur begat Mathan.
And Mathan begat Jacob.
And Jacob begat Joseph.

OLD PEOPLE

There is now a line of old people facing the audience at the front of the stage. They speak out a name or two, or mumble, from the many names of the "begatting." The four women of the chorus are davenning without words. The other actresses, the ones who have just played the mothers, are at the back of the stage, and they davenn, too, softly.

THE SONG

The actors move about freely on the stage. Each is overtaken by a slow kind of dying, not so much a physical one as a kind of "emptying out," a living death, which soon slows them to a complete stop. Each actor has a final small physical tremor. Then, as if ghosts, the actors begin to sing a sentimental popular song from twenty or thirty years ago. No longer as ghosts but as themselves they continue singing the song as they leave the theater, walking out through the audience.

JEAN-CLAUDE van ITALLIE

Jean-Claude van Itallie was born in Brussels in 1936. He was raised on Long Island, in Great Neck, and graduated from Harvard in 1958. He joined the Open Theater when it started, in 1963. In November 1966 his *America Hurrah* opened at the Pocket Theater in New York and ran there for over one and a half years. It has since been produced, hailed, and banned all over the world.

THE OPEN THEATER

In 1963 a group of actors and directors and playwrights in downtown New York found themselves at the same point in their professional development—tired of conventional New York theatrical expression, and disgusted with the nearly total lack of outlets available for experimental work. This group, headed by Joseph Chaikin, became the Open Theater. The nucleus of the group is the same five years later. And their dialogue continues about what is worth expressing in the theater, and how to express it. The Open Theater has been deliberately non-commercial. Rent on the rehearsal loft has been paid by members' dues. But the Open Theater has, since its beginning, performed one- or two-night programs of short plays and improvisations in nearly every off and off-off Broadway house. And its effect on all phases of avant-garde American theater, to quote the *Village Voice*, "has been seminal." *The Serpent* is the first piece to be built fully as a collaborative work within and by the Open Theater. It is the result of several months' unpaid, full-time commitment, and countless discussions and improvisations on the part of the eighteen actors and the other artists involved. *The Serpent* was taken to Europe by the Open Theater in the summer of 1968, and it was enthusiastically received there by audiences and critics in Italy, Switzerland, Germany and Denmark.

JOSEPH CHAIKIN

Joseph Chaikin, founder of the Open Theater, is thirty-two years old. He was born in Brooklyn of Russian parents, and he went to school at Drake University in Iowa. He was for several years the central actor of the Living Theater, with which the Open Theater has continued to exchange ideas over the years. Chaikin has won several off-Broadway "Obies," including one for his performance in Brecht's *Man Is Man*.

56

PROPERTIES

Simple musical instruments, for procession
Bag of apples

A FABLE

A Collaborative Piece

NOTE ON MUSIC

A piano-vocal score containing the songs and music composed by Richard Peaslee for the original production of A FABLE can be purchased from the Play Service at a price of $8.00 per set, plus postage. Any nonprofessional group authorized to give a production of this play may, upon purchase of the aforementioned piano-vocal score, make use of the songs and music contained in the performance without the payment of an additional royalty, as the use of the songs and music is included in the royalty quoted for performance of the play itself.

A FABLE

A Collaborative Piece
Written by
Jean-Claude van Itallie

Music composed by
Richard Peaslee

Originally created collaboratively with
Director: Joseph Chaikin

And actors:

JOYCE AARON: Afflicted Person, Grandmother

SHAMI CHAIKIN: Dreamer's Interpreter, Ghost

BERNARD DUFFY: Puppeteer, Fugitive

MURRAY MOSS: Person Hiding Under a Stone

TINA SHEPARD: Journeyor

MARGO LEE SHERMAN: Puppeteer, Hanging Person

CHARLES STANLEY: King

PAUL ZIMET: Hermit, Treebeast, Dreamer

ARTISTIC ADVISOR: Mira Rafalowicz

PRODUCTION MANAGER: Jon Teta

LIGHTING DESIGNER: Arden Fingerhut

ASSISTANT-TO-THE-PLAYWRIGHT: Rosemary Quinn

ADMINISTRATION: Jane Yockel

PRESS: David Roggensack

This piece was conceived during the summer of 1974. Work with the actors began in February, 1975. The first performance was at Lenox, Massachusetts at the Lenox Arts Festival at Wheatleigh (Lyn Austin, producer). After ten days of open rehearsal "A Fable" opened in New York City at the Exchange Theatre in the Westbeth Artists Housing Building on October 18, 1975, again sponsored by the Lenox Arts Festival.

The long development periods were made possible by grants from the National Endowment for the Arts, the New York State Council on the Arts, and the Ostrow and Shubert Foundations

3

PRODUCTION NOTE

The Marketplace scene and the Last Scene of the Play, both almost totally non-verbal, will clearly vary from production to production. What is provided here is a skeletal outline based on the original production. There must be no *verbal* improvisation, however, in either of these scenes or in any other part of the play.

A FABLE

The physical production is simple. It looks as if it could be carried around by a troupe of traveling performers. Upstage Center is a high "box" made of scaffolding. Its sides are curtained with brown burlap. There is a similarly made box Downstage Right. It is lower than the other and has a small platform in front of it. Stage Left is an area for the musicians, and next to them a singing area for the actors. A wire is stretched across the front of the stage from the musicians to the box on the Right. From it hang several panels of burlap: the "curtain." There are some portable units which are moved by the actors between scenes: two three-tiered sets of steps, a smaller two-step unit, and a couple of stools.

The costumes are well worn and part of the everyday wear of the performers. The materials are cotton and soft; the cut has no particular ethnic suggestion; the colors are earth colors. A particular piece of clothing will be used sometimes for a particular scene: a black top for the Ghost, a green top for the Hermit.

The lighting is mostly white and doesn't change much. Singing is done by the actors who also occasionally play a musical instrument. Music will sometimes accompany or punctuate the action and words.

The actors are in the first row of the audience in seats to which they will sometimes return. The play begins when the actors rise and go to the singing area.

SONG:
The Fable
When did it happen?
Once upon a time that was not this time.
Where did it start?
In the Village of People Who Fish in the Lake.

Once upon a time
In the Village of People Who Fish in the Lake

5

They were repairing the net
But forgot that the lake was dry.

Once upon a time
In the Village of People Who Fish in the Lake
They were having a meeting
But forgot that they were meeting.

Once upon a time
In the Village of People Who Fish in the Lake
They chose a villager to go for help
But forgot who they were sending.

Once upon a time
In the Village of People Who Fish in the Lake
They talked of the Golden Time
But only knew
That this was not it.

(*The actors leave the singing area and group themselves around and on the two larger stair units, facing the audience. They pick up the net and a few materials with which to repair it. All the announcements in the piece are made by the actors when they are ready to proceed with the next scene. There is a "ping" of music before each announcement and a percussion sound after.*)

ANNOUNCEMENT: The Village of People Who Fish in the Lake
(*They begin to work on repairing the net. They work rhythmically but their rhythm is interrupted as one or the other forgets what they are doing, they "gap." They have three modes of speaking and moving together. The first is the "busy" mode, which is rapid.*)
7TH VILLAGER. Measure it out. Take it.
1ST VILLAGER. Not in the middle.
8TH VILLAGER. Take it. I've got it.
6TH VILLAGER. Stretch the net. Over here.
5TH VILLAGER. Hold the end.
2ND VILLAGER. Toss.
(*They switch into the "work" mode which is more methodical.*)
1ST VILLAGER. Stitch. Stitch.
2ND VILLAGER. Toss, toss.
1ST VILLAGER. Stitch. Stitch.

2ND VILLAGER. Toss, toss.

3RD VILLAGER. Hold it.

4TH VILLAGER. I *am* holding it.

1ST VILLAGER. Stitch. Stitch.

2ND VILLAGER. Toss, toss.

3RD VILLAGER. Hold it.

4TH VILLAGER. I *am* holding it.

5TH VILLAGER. Shuttle.

(*They enter the "interrupted" mode of almost remembering that they are having a meeting.*)

1ST VILLAGER. A——

7TH VILLAGER. Wasn't there a ——

6TH VILLAGER. Didn't someone?

1ST VILLAGER. A——

3RD VILLAGER. Didn't you——?

8TH VILLAGER. I thought we were——

1ST VILLAGER. A——

2ND VILLAGER. The lake has——

1ST VILLAGER. A——

6TH VILLAGER. You started to say that—

1ST VILLAGER. A——

4TH VILLAGER. We sent somebody——

7TH VILLAGER. There was a message to——

8TH VILLAGER. We have to decide on——

2ND VILLAGER. What did he just say?

1ST VILLAGER. She said that——

6TH VILLAGER. A——

(*The 5th Villager goes to the side and whispers to the 6th Villager to come and lie down with her and rest, which he does as the others continue to work.*)

5TH VILLAGER. Pssst. Come here.

6TH VILLAGER. What?

5TH VILLAGER. Pssst. Come lie down over here.

(*The others are still busy.*)

7TH VILLAGER. Measure it out. Measure it out.

1ST VILLAGER. Not in the middle.

8TH VILLAGER. Take it.

2ND VILLAGER. Toss.

(*Again, they almost remember something. The 5th Villager without being very aware of what she is doing puts a soft cloth*) *pack on the back of the 3rd Villager. The 3rd Villager adjusts the pack and continues to work on the net.)*

5TH VILLAGER. Wasn't there a ——

4TH VILLAGER. The meeting is——

8TH VILLAGER. Ask the king to——

6TH VILLAGER. Didn't someone——

1ST VILLAGER. A——

2ND VILLAGER. Wasn't someone leaving?

8TH VILLAGER. The meeting——

1ST VILLAGER. A——

7TH VILLAGER. Something happened to the——

4TH VILLAGER. We should have——

1ST VILLAGER. A——

(As the others work rapidly again the 5th Villager goes to the other side of the stage and again calls the 6th Villager to lie down and rest with her.)

7TH VILLAGER. Measure it out. Measure it out.

5TH VILLAGER. Pssst. Come here.

1ST VILLAGER. Not in the middle.

6TH VILLAGER. What?

8TH VILLAGER. Take it.

2ND VILLAGER. Toss.

5TH VILLAGER. Psst. Come lie down over here.

(As the villagers work a couple of them get up and wave good-bye to someone, but they are not sure whom. A couple of others embrace.)

1ST VILLAGER. Stitch. Stitch.

2ND VILLAGER. Toss, toss.

3RD VILLAGER. Hold it.

4TH VILLAGER. I *am* holding it.

5TH VILLAGER. Shuttle!

6TH VILLAGER. Watch the seam. Pull the edge.

1ST VILLAGER. Stitch. Stitch.

2ND VILLAGER. Toss, toss.

3RD VILLAGER. Hold it.

4TH VILLAGER. I *am* holding it.

5TH VILLAGER. Shuttle!

6TH VILLAGER. Watch the seam, pull the edge.

7TH VILLAGER. Turn, turn.

(The 3rd Villager, the one with the pack on, leaves, as if going

to look for someone. She does not come back. The others don't
seem to miss her. Once again they almost remember that they are
meeting.)
6TH VILLAGER. Didn't someone——
1ST VILLAGER. A——
2ND VILLAGER. Wasn't someone——
8TH VILLAGER. The meeting——
    (Then they return to work.)
1ST VILLAGER. Stitch. Stitch.
2ND VILLAGER. Toss, toss.
5TH VILLAGER. Shuttle!
6TH VILLAGER. Watch the seam. Pull the edge.

ANNOUNCEMENT: The Golden Time

(They are remembering, as they work on the net, what they
were told of the Golden Time. There is a musical accompaniment,
but the Litany is not a song.)
2ND VILLAGER. In the Golden Time
In the Golden Time
Everything was exactly as it is today,
they say.
1ST VILLAGER. Only
6TH VILLAGER. There were no differences between places then.
8TH VILLAGER. Of course there were differences.
5TH VILLAGER. But people moved dancing.
And people spoke music.
2ND VILLAGER. Everything was exactly as it is today.
1ST VILLAGER. Only
7TH VILLAGER. There were no boundaries then.
8TH VILLAGER. Of course there were boundaries.
2ND VILLAGER. Everything was exactly as it is today.
1ST VILLAGER. Only
7TH VILLAGER. There were no frontiers in the Golden Time
8TH VILLAGER. There *were* frontiers
In the Golden Time.
2ND VILLAGER. Everything was exactly as it is today,
they say.
1ST VILLAGER. Only
6TH VILLAGER. There were no alarm clocks then.
8TH VILLAGER. There *were* alarm clocks then.

9

7TH VILLAGER. There were alarm clocks but there was no terror.
8TH VILLAGER. Of course there was terror.
4TH VILLAGER. But there was no fear.
8TH VILLAGER. Of course there was fear.
2ND VILLAGER. Everything was exactly as it is today,
they say.
1ST VILLAGER. Only
7TH VILLAGER. A tomato was a tomato.
6TH VILLAGER. Blue was blue.
7TH VILLAGER. There was no disagreement.
8TH VILLAGER. There *was* disagreement.
7TH VILLAGER. There was no disagreement.
8TH VILLAGER. There *was* disagreement.
1ST VILLAGER. Only
5TH VILLAGER. People moved dancing
And people spoke music.
2ND VILLAGER. Yes.
6TH VILLAGER. There was no money
In the Golden Time.
8TH VILLAGER. Of course there was money.
7TH VILLAGER. But money didn't matter so much in those days,
they say.
2ND VILLAGER. Everything was exactly as it is today.
1ST VILLAGER. Only
6TH VILLAGER. Pain was pain.
5TH VILLAGER. People moved dancing and people spoke music.
1ST VILLAGER. Only
6TH VILLAGER. Everything was familiar.
7TH VILLAGER. Everything was amazing.
5TH VILLAGER. Everything was familiar and amazing at once,
they say.
1ST VILLAGER. Only
7TH VILLAGER. There was no yearning.
8TH VILLAGER. There *was* yearning.
7TH VILLAGER. There was no yearning.
8TH VILLAGER. There *was* yearning.
1ST VILLAGER. Only
4TH VILLAGER. No one yearned for the Golden Time for this
was it.
2ND VILLAGER. Everything was exactly as it is today, they say.

1ST VILLAGER. Only

5TH VILLAGER. People spoke music

And people moved dancing.

2ND VILLAGER. Yes.

6TH VILLAGER. But there was no king.

8TH VILLAGER. Of course there was a king.

6TH VILLAGER. But there was no king.

8TH VILLAGER. Of course there was a king.

(*Repeating himself although no one disagreed this time.*)

Of course there was a king.

1ST VILLAGER. Only

7TH VILLAGER. Everyone ruled themselves in the Golden Time.

2ND VILLAGER. In the Golden Time everything was much as it is today.

1ST VILLAGER. Only

5TH VILLAGER. People spoke music

And people moved dancing.

4TH VILLAGER. Everything was familiar and amazing at once, they say.

6TH VILLAGER. And people saw color.

5TH VILLAGER. And people moved dancing.

And people spoke music.

2ND VILLAGER. Yes.

Everything was exactly the same as it is today, they say.

1ST VILLAGER. Only

5TH VILLAGER. People moved dancing

And people spoke music

2ND VILLAGER. In the Golden Time

Everything was exactly as it is today, they say.

1ST VILLAGER. Only

5TH VILLAGER. People moved dancing.

People spoke music.

2ND VILLAGER. Everything was exactly the same as it is today, they say.

1ST VILLAGER. Only.

ANNOUNCEMENT: (*Made by the 3rd Villager who has now become the Journeyor.*)

The Beginning of the Journey

(*The Journeyor has climbed to the top of the scaffolding of the side box, she sways slightly to the music of the song.*)

11

SONG:

And so the journeyor left the Village
   of People Who Fish in the Lake and
Journeyed to the King of the Country
   of People Who Fish in the Lake
To find out what was wrong.

In the small courtyard of the palace
She saw hundreds of people.

They seemed strange
As if they had seen something terrible.

There was a smell.
The journeyor knew
Something had passed through the courtyard.
(*There is quick journeying music on the marimba as the plat-forms are rearranged to look like the steps of the palace.*)

ANNOUNCEMENT: In Front of the King's Palace
The Courtyard of the Afflicted.
(*There are several afflicted persons in the Courtyard. One woman is pushing a heavy broom in a constant back and forth motion. Then she pulls her own hair straight up and speaks:*)
AFFLICTED PERSON. In the middle of the night
I am hidden.
In the middle of the night
I am cold.
In the middle of the night
There is screaming
But no face.
In the middle of the night
I hold my breath
But there is no house.
In the middle of the night
The light is bright
But there is no seeing.
In the middle of the night:
No fingers
No mouth
No ears
No sister

12

In the middle of the night
There is crying
But no child.

(*The Journeyor goes under the steps and crawls slowly toward the other side. A woman is scrubbing the steps making small high-pitched moaning sounds. A man with a bucket and a washboard suddenly begins to make masturbating motions over everything he can find, including the armless sleeve of the man kneeling on the two-step unit. Then he calms down but the limbless man begins to make inarticulate angry sounds. Another man is clutching his own shirt as if with a disembodied hand. The woman scrubbing makes louder high-pitched noises. The Journeyor is fascinated but frightened. Then she is through the Courtyard. The musicians play the introduction of the last song at a fast tempo. The curtain is pulled by the Journeyor and pushed by another actor immediately after so that it has traveled across the stage but is still open. The king sits on top of the high box. His head is between his knees. He sits up with a groan. Some of what he says is accompanied by the viola.*)

ANNOUNCEMENT: The King

KING. We are our kingdom.
We are our forests, our deer and our bear,
Our cities and our insects.
Our body is the body of our country.
We are the mouth of our people.
They moan with our voice.
We are king of the afflicted,
And we are afflicted.
We are king of dry fields,
And our throat is parched.
There is famine and the king grows thin.
Invasion —— the king bleeds.
The enemy takes our towns: the king's canker grows.
Fires; the king is enfevered.
Bridges collapse; the king's veins rupture.

(*He sits up higher and groans again.*)

Our treasury has no value.
Our soldiers are weak and dispersed
Our generals are old.

13

Our doctors have no remedies.
Our counselors are stupid.
(*He sits in a more relaxed inviting manner.*)
Not many get through our courtyard.
We are lonely here.
We offer you half our kingdom and half our crown
If you will sit and play chess with us.
(*The Journeyor climbs up some steps and for a moment stands in front of the King. Then she changes her mind and jumps down.*)
JOURNEYOR. No!
KING. (*Angrily.*) We could have you beaten
Imprisoned, or hanged
But——
We will give you a task to accomplish
And if you do not accomplish it,
Your life will be forfeit.
JOURNEYOR. What is the task?
KING. The beast.
It has closed up our ports.
It has dried up our lakes.
It has sent pestilence to our villages.
It has afflicted the people in our courtyard.
It has hidden the harvest and stolen the seeds.
JOURNEYOR. What is the task?
KING. You must kill the beast.
JOURNEYOR. Kill it?
KING. Stab it, burn it, hit it, or trick it
But kill it.
Then bring us back its claws
And we will give you one to plant in your village
And the Golden Time will be again.
JOURNEYOR. What is this beast?
KING. That is your task.
JOURNEYOR. How shall I recognize it?
KING. That is your task.
JOURNEYOR. Where shall I find it?
KING. That is your task.
The king tends to the kingdom.
The audience is over.
(*The king leans forward with a groan, his face hidden again.*

14

There is music from the next song while the curtain is pulled the other way and the stair units are put back to back and a burlap-covered board placed on top of them. During the song the Journeyor sits on this board as if watching the sea. Then she lies down to sleep, using her pack for a pillow.)

SONG:

And then the journeyor left the king
And journeyed through all the villages of the kingdom
Until she reached the end.
And then she crossed the border
Into a country
Where they speak another language.

And then she asked directions.

And then the journeyor journeyed
Until the days were short.

And then she saw the sea.

And then the journeyor sat
And watched the sun rise
And watched the shadows rise
And watched the clouds pass
And watched the night come
And watched the stars come.

And then the journeyor was cold and went to sleep.

And then she dreamt of what she'd seen.
And then awoke quick.
The stone had moved under her head.

(As the Journeyor sleeps a periscope comes slowly up from under the platform and looks around. When it sights the Journeyor it quickly jumps back under. The Journeyor wakes up. A hand pushes up a round part of the board on which the Journeyor was sleeping. The Journeyor grabs the piece of board and tries to tug it up. There is a tussle with a person we can't yet see.)

PERSON HIDING UNDER THE STONE. Stop it.
Leave me alone.

(The "stone" is back in place. The Journeyor cleverly pries it up suddenly. She pulls it and her pack away and jumps behind the

15

platform. An arm comes up and feels around for the missing piece of stone. Then, slowly the head of a person appears.)

PERSON. I live here to be hidden, unnoticed, forgotten.
Leave me alone.

JOURNEYOR. Tell me about the beast.

(Journeyor hides behind the platform.)

PERSON. Look out its not in the house.
Look out its not in the road.
Look out its not in the meal.
Look out its not inside you.
Look out its not in the words.

JOURNEYOR. Tell me about the beast.

PERSON. When you see it you run
You run and you run and you run and you run
And you look out its not in the running.
You find a stone to hide under
And you look out its not in the stone. Sh.

(As he speaks there are two "remembered" people on stage. The woman from the Courtyard who spoke appears in front of the D. R. *box, pulling her hair up and moving her lips but without sound. Another person from the Courtyard sits on the two-step unit very slowly putting her head into her knees and looking up again.)*

It'll appear unexpectedly
When you've just begun to feel safe:
In a familiar face,
In the body of a lover,
In a soup,
In what you see through a telescope.

It has no eyes of its own.
It takes over people.
It becomes places:
A smile where no smile belongs.
Something inside you know is not yourself:
That is the beast!

(The drummer beats a quick hard beat.)

Suddenly what was familiar is unfamiliar.
That is the beast. Sh.

(Another beat on the drum. Both the Person Hiding Under the Stone and the Journeyor are frightened by what is being said. The

16

Journeyor's head sometimes disappears behind the platform. The Person's head sometimes disappears under it.)
It comes sometimes when you talk about it,
Sometimes when you avoid it.
You'll recognize it in the body of someone who's just seen it.
It watches with the eyes of those who watch it.
Listen. I'll tell you what happened:
I come from the Village of Messengers:
A sudden scream in the middle of the night.
An army of claws attacking,
A strange sick smell,
The beast's smile,
And the rest of the night: silence.
In the morning
I am shivering,
Alone in the beast's cold,
Where before the climate had been hot,
Where before there had been my village.

Now when I am disturbed I move.
I intend to find some other stone,
More ordinary,
Heavier,
Which no one will suspect.
JOURNEYOR. Tell me about the beast.
(The Person Hiding Under the Stone has disappeared again, this time for good. The Journeyor carefully replaces the lid. Accompanied by journeying music she crosses in front of the curtain as it is closed by another actor. A sawed-off piece of tree trunk is placed in front of the box D. R. The Hermit sits on it. He wears a green top and a rag over his face with eye-holes in it.)

ANNOUNCEMENT: The Story of the Hermit who Lives in the
Middle of the Woods
(The Hermit has a gravelly voice. He pulls off his mask.)
HERMIT. I was born in the Village Where People Buy and Sell
  Bones.
But I never felt at home there.
I tried to like the people,
And I wanted them to admire me.

17

For many years I worked very hard.
I had a family.

I became rich.
I built a house.
Everyone envied me.
They thought I must be the happiest man in the world.
Still I did not feel at home in the Village of People Who Buy and
    Sell Bones.
It seemed impossible to imagine living anywhere else,
But it became impossible to stay.
One day I left.
All I could think of was the people I had left behind.
And it hurt me, it hurt me.
I kept on traveling.
But no village seemed to me any better than the one I had left.
And no people seemed to me any better
Than the people who buy and sell bones.
So I went into the woods,
Into the deepest part of the woods.
And I stayed there.
I built a hut.
At first I was lonely.
I thought of growing old and dying in the woods.
I was afraid of meeting the beast alone in the woods.
One night I looked at the stars.
They seemed so distant.
That made me feel calm.
I began to like the woods.
I began to make music.
My skin became like bark.
My fingers became like roots.
Moss and fungus grew on my face.
To others I became hideous,
But not to myself.
Every once in a while
Someone who was lost in the woods came to my hut
But my voice and my body frightened them
And they ran away.

There was the year a hunter came and burned down my hut and I
　　had to build it again.
There was a year when the woods were filled with owls.
There were many years I didn't count.
And then

*(The Hermit moves behind the curtain of the box, taking the
stump with him, while the Puppeteers, two of them, each with a
puppet, come out and kneel on the platform.)*

ANNOUNCEMENT: The Puppet Show

*(The Journeyor sits on the floor at the corner of the platform,
fascinated by the Puppeteers.)*

SHE. Let's tell the story of the first moment when you're born.

HE. No. I don't know it. How about——

SHE. What?

HE. The story of the very last moment which hasn't happened yet.

SHE No. I don't want to.

How about the story which if you hear it will change your life

Do you know it?

HE. No.

SHE. Neither do I.

HE. What about the one about the village?

SHE. Which village?

HE. The village where they forgot everything.

SHE. All right.

One morning I woke up and forgot I was awake.

HE. No. It starts like this:

Once upon a time that was not this time——

SHE. And then what happened?

HE. Then she went to the king.

SHE. Am I the king?

HE. No.

SHE. Well get to my part.

And then what happened?

HE. And then she had a dream.

SHE. She dreamed of a dish of cream as wide as a lake.

HE. No.

SHE. And then she jumped into the cream and she drank it all up.

HE. No. In the village there was a mother and a father and they
　　had a family.

And they all lived happily ever after.

SHE. Except that one of them got lost.

HE. Yes. And he had to kill the dragon.

SHE. Yes, and that's how he won the princess.

And at the wedding they had cream and berries and soup and cake
and everybody had some.

HE. And they danced.

SHE. Let's tell the story of the wedding and the princess and the
prince after they killed the dragon and the king said it would be
all right.

HE. We just did.

SHE. But not in the right order. We have to put the beginning before the end

And all the middle parts in the middle.

HE. All right. One morning he woke up in the village

And he hugged his mother

And she gave him some things to take with him.

And everybody said goodbye.

SHE. No, nobody said goodbye to anybody.

She left all by herself

And when she got to the king he told her to save the prince from a
fate worse than death.

HE. What's a fate worse than death?

SHE. I don't know

But she was courageous and honest and clever
and brave and strong and had all the magic weapons

And so she killed the dragon

And they had half the kingdom
until the king died
and then they had the whole thing.

And children.

And they lived happily ever after.

And that's the right story in the right order.

HE. And then what happened?

SHE. And then she walked and walked and walked and walked—

HE. And found the hermit who lived in the middle of the woods.

SHE. Yes, but she wasn't scared.

HE. No.

SHE. And then what happened?

HE. And then he went to see his grandmother.

20

SHE. She was four hundred and six years old.
HE. And then what happened?
SHE. And then she came to the marketplace
And she saw the puppetshow.
JOURNEYOR. And then what happened?

(*They look at her an instant, then go quickly behind the curtain.*)

ANNOUNCEMENT: The Marketplace of Buying and Selling

(*The Marketplace is a series of overlapping images. The actors come out through the curtains to present an image, or a line of them, to the audience, then go behind the curtain again. The rhythm from the musicians and from the actors, however, is constant, and the stage is never empty. The first is the Charm Seller. He sits quickly and twirls a pair of black spangled ribbons around his head.*)

CHARM SELLER. Charms to ward off evil.
Cures to keep the beast from your door.

(*He remains seated as the Blind Beggar, her eyes rolled back in her head, using a stick, crosses the stage. The Magician appears repeating constantly a hand-under-leg movement and repeating some hawking sounds. A Concertina Player plays. From behind the curtain a male Hustler leers invitingly. From another panel of the curtain a Head sticks its tongue out at us. An actress repeats a single tired motion, as if standing around on the street on one foot then the other. A Fluteplayer. A hand moves slowly from the curtain and is clapped over a man's face. A Couple stand staring at the audience. She is frightened. He is snarling. A couple of Finger Magicians perform a quick trick that pleases them very much. They bow. A head bobs over the top of the curtain, crossing the stage. A pair of hands dances under one panel of the curtain. Another pair of hands dances under another panel. A pair of feet dance under a third panel. A man steps out and slowly lifts a piece of cloth covering him. At crotch level another head is revealed, its tongue out, leering. A Juggler juggles. The Blind Beggar crosses the stage again. A couple of performers in green watch caps come out. He plays the flute. She dances wildly. They both put out their caps for some money. The Couple from the Village appear dreamily, swaying. Two men demonstrate a Vibrating Dance, one lying, one standing. The Beggar crosses again. Two Fiddlers play. Two men dance on*)

21

the platform in front of the box R. *Two people dance in a more bouncy manner on the other side. The Blind Beggar remains on stage. The Concertina Player comes back. The Charm Seller is back in place. So is the Magician. The Hustler appears again. Suddenly the Beast appears in all of them. The concertina makes only a breathing sound. The Blind Beggar appears to be seeing and leering. The Charm Seller is silent, as is the music, and suddenly hisses violently. Now the Magician starts making her sound and her movement again, and all goes slowly back to normal. The Journeyor has been observing the entire Marketplace, and is frightened.)*

ANNOUNCEMENT: Running From the Beast,
Resting Under a Tree

(The Journeyor is running, accompanied by a drumroll, and throws herself under the Tree. The actor playing the Tree stands on a sawed-off piece of tree trunk which the Hermit sat on. He holds his fingers and arms in the air like branches. His breathing is audible, like wind in the branches. Then the winds start to be accompanied by a slight clicking sound in the voice. The Journeyor becomes concerned. When the Tree begins to speak she knows it is the voice of the Beast, but she is too frightened to move.)

TREEBEAST. I can numb you,

Grow inside you,

I can isolate you from all living beings,

I can make your teeth soft,

Make you sleepless,

Make you think my thoughts,

Suffocate you,

I can grow inside you,

Become your body,

Become your eyes,

Become any being you see,

Or I can ignore you always.

(Attempting to kill the Beast the Journeyor chops down the Tree and the actor playing it lays on the ground. The Beast is no longer evident, only a fallen tree. The Journeyor runs rapidly to each corner of the stage.)

JOURNEYOR. And then?

And then?

And then?

And then?
And then?
And then?
   (*The curtain is opened and closed.*)

ANNOUNCEMENT: The Island of the Better Than Golden Time
   (*The First Person enters, crosses to* c. *and announces her character.*)
FIRST PERSON. The Person Who Before Was Always Startled
   (*She demonstrates physically as the Second Person, and then the others in turn, announce themselves and demonstrate too.*)
SECOND PERSON. The Person Whose Parts Had Always Escaped Him
THIRD PERSON. The Person Who Couldn't Make Up His Mind
FOURTH PERSON. The Person Who Couldn't Stop Hiding
FIFTH PERSON. The Person To Whom the World Smelled of Dead Fish
SIXTH PERSON. The Person Who Couldn't Stop Speaking
SEVENTH PERSON. The Person Who Couldn't Stop Crying
JOURNEYOR. The Person Who Couldn't Stop Laughing At The Person Who Couldn't Stop Crying.
   (*The last two, the Crying Person and the Laughing Journeyor, sit together at* c. *All are demonstrating their characters.*)
FOURTH PERSON. But now that they lived on the Island of the
   Better Than Golden Time
The Person Who Before Was Always Startled
was never surprised by anything.
   (*The First Person demonstrates her new calm and then makes the next announcement.*)
FIRST PERSON. The Person Whose Parts Had Always Escaped Him was now collected and calm.
   (*The Second Person demonstrates his new calm and makes the next announcement, and so on in turn.*)
SECOND PERSON. The Person Who Could Never Make Up His Mind was now a leader.
THIRD PERSON. The Person Who Could Never Stop Hiding now came out into the sun.
FOURTH PERSON. The Person to Whom the World Smelled of Dead Fish now smelled only flowers.

23

FIFTH PERSON. The Person Who Couldn't Stop Crying was now the one with the largest smile.

SIXTH PERSON. The Person Who Couldn't Stop Speaking, did.

(There is a dissonant cymbal crash from the musicians.)

SONG.

And then she traveled alone
For a long time.
And then she saw a person hanging
And she cut her down.
And then they looked for the beast together
To bring about the Golden Time.

ANNOUNCEMENT: The Hanging Person

(In the box at the back of the stage a person is seen hanging. The actress playing the Hanging Person carries a small home-made rag doll at her waist; she holds the jump rope from which she is hanging. The Journeyor sees the Hanging Person. She rushes up and cuts her down.)

JOURNEYOR. What happened? Was it the beast?

(The Journeyor cradles the Hanging Person in her arms.)

HANGING PERSON. I don't want my body anymore.

I don't want to feed it.
I don't want to work to feed it.
I don't want to dream.
I don't want to wake up.
I don't want to give birth to children.
I don't want to run away.
I don't want to stand still.
I want to stop my battle with the ground.

JOURNEYOR. Then wait until I'm gone.

(The Journeyor begins to climb down from the box.)

But if I go——

(She stops.)

No, I can't leave you.

(She helps the Hanging Person climb down from the box. They both sit on the ground. The Journeyor takes off her pack.)

HANGING PERSON. I traveled a long way from the City of the Thousand Foot Towers,

Then you cut me down.
Now you won't leave me.

But when you've forgotten what I'm going to do
I'll slip away and do it.
JOURNEYOR. Do you want some water?
HANGING PERSON. I don't want to drink.
  (*The Journeyor passes her a water bottle.*)
JOURNEYOR. Here.
HANGING PERSON. Thank you, but I'm not grateful.
JOURNEYOR. I've been traveling a long time.
HANGING PERSON. Who asked you to travel?
Why don't you stop?
JOURNEYOR. Stop and do what?
Shall we sleep now?
HANGING PERSON. Yes, let's sleep.
  (*They hold hands and, remaining seated, each bends from the waist in the same direction, and they go to sleep.*)
SONG.
  The Journeyor from the Village of People
    Who Fish in the Lake, fish in the lake
  And the journeyor who had been hanging, hanging
  Traveled together for a while.

  The Journeyor from the Village of People
    Who Fish in the Lake, fish in the lake
  And the Journeyor who had been hanging, hanging
  Traveled together for a while.

  Then they heard about the dreamer
  Who knew about the beast
  And they traveled together.
  (*The Journeyor and the Hanging Person climb the scaffolding of the side box to listen to the Dreamer.*)

ANNOUNCEMENT: The Dreamer Who Never Wakes Up
  (*The Dreamer, bare-chested, is led by the hand by an Interpreter. The Dreamer stands in the middle of the stage. He makes a slight rasping sound in his throat, accompanied by a barely audible ringing sound from the musicians. We will see the dreams in the Dreamer's body. We will hear the dreams through the Interpreter's voice. The Interpreter sits on the ground L. facing the Dreamer.*)
INTERPRETER. I'm lying in the meadow.

I'm moving with my shadow in the meadow.
Now my shadow has become solid.
It has become a house.
I'm dreaming I'm waking in the house.
I'm grasping at the walls.
I see the meadow has become a picture on the wall.
I know I'm dreaming but I can't stop.
JOURNEYOR. That is the beast!

(*There is a short hard drumbeat whenever the phrase "That is the beast" is repeated. The Hanging Person has slipped away out of the side box. The Dreamer's foot begins to twitch violently.*)

INTERPRETER. I am walking in the City of Beggars.
A beggar with no feet is sitting on the ground.
He grabs my foot.
He will not let go.
JOURNEYOR. That is the beast!

(*We see in the body of the Dreamer the arrival of the rat.*)

INTERPRETER. I am in the Village with Rats.
A rat comes and bites me.
I give the rat my food.
The rat comes again.
I give the rat everyone's food.
The rat comes again.
The rat is fatter.
I give the rat my body.
The rat comes again.
JOURNEYOR. That is the beast!

(*Just as the Interpreter next begins to speak the Hanging Person is entering the box at the back.*)

INTERPRETER. Now someone is entering the dream.
I see them in the distance.
Now they are close by.
Now we are touching.
Now they are far away again.
Now there is no love.
JOURNEYOR. That is the beast!

(*By now the Hanging Person has hung herself again.*)

INTERPRETER. I'm standing in a white room,
Standing for a long time.
Suddenly my own head falls and breaks on the ground.

26

(The Dreamer starts making the sound he made when he entered.)

And out of the two parts of my skull
I see the beast coming toward me.

(The drum roll again. The Dreamer stops making his tiny screaming sound when the Interpreter takes him by the hand. But he continues the sound as he is led off. The Journeyor is astraddle the scaffolding on top of the side box. She faces the audience, speaks with vigor, rocking back and forth, each sentence punctuated by a single beat of the drum.)

JOURNEYOR. The beast is in the fog.

The beast is in the soup.

The beast is in the feast.

The beast is in the soldiers.

The beast is in the skull.

The beast is in the king.

The beast is in the stone.

The beast is in the beggar.

The beast is in the child.

The beast is in the dream.

(The Journeyor sings the next song from where she is. The others are in the singing area.)

SONG.

The beast is in the fog.

The beast is in the soup.

The beast is in the feast.

The beast is in the soldiers.

The beast is in the skull.

The beast is in the king.

The beast is in the stone.

The beast is in the beggar.

The beast is in the child.

The beast is in the dream.

(The Journeyor climbs down. She notices the Hanging Person Hanging. There is nothing to do this time. The actress playing the Hanging Person closes the curtain of the box. Tympani music accompanies the Journeyor as she climbs into the scaffolding of the side box. The actress removes the pack and any costume encumbrances to the gymnastic physicality of the next scene. An actor is

27

in the scaffolding under the center box. He makes the next announcement.)

ANNOUNCEMENT: The Fugitive Who Killed The King
(The Journeyor and the Fugitive eye each other, each from under their scaffolding.)
JOURNEYOR. What are you hiding from?
Is it the beast?
FUGITIVE. I'm running from the palace of the king.
I was a slave.
(The Journeyor and the Fugitive are in the c. playing area on all fours. The two-step unit is between them. Their tone is urgent, and each time that one or the other start to speak they both move positions quickly, as people in hiding.)
JOURNEYOR. I didn't see slaves there.
FUGITIVE. There are thousands
Under the king's floors,
Behind the king's walls.
Slaves cook the king's meals
Polish the king's weapons
Tend the king's sleep.
Only the king has the right to privacy.
The beast is in the king.
JOURNEYOR. The beast is in the king!
FUGITIVE. But the king doesn't see it.
In the palace only the slaves see the beast.
JOURNEYOR. But the king sent me to kill the beast,
To bring back its claws!
FUGITIVE. The king was a liar.
He told you "get claws"
So you would believe there were claws.
He told you "kill it"
So you would believe it could be killed.
But the beast has no claws.
It can't be killed.
In the palace we killed the king.
JOURNEYOR. You killed the king!
FUGITIVE. But there was still the beast.
We put a doll on the throne
But there was still the beast.

28

We destroyed the doll
But there was still the beast.
JOURNEYOR. In my village we need help.
In my village they are forgetting.
FUGITIVE. But if the beast has no claws,
If the beast can't be killed——
JOURNEYOR. Still, I have to find the beast
Whatever it is,
Or isn't.
FUGITIVE. If I go home I'll be killed.
I'm a fugitive.
I can't go back.
I'll journey with you.
JOURNEYOR. I'll journey with you.
   (*The Journeyor and the Fugitive travel together, the Journeyor
on the Fugitive's back, as if swimming in slow motion.*)
SONG.
   The journeyor and the fugitive
   Remained together a long time.
   They became traveling storytellers.
   They never stayed long in one place.
   Sometimes they stole,
   Sometimes performed tricks.
   They stayed a while in the City of the Thousand Foot Towers,
   Traveled to the Country Where the People Eat their Dead.
   The journeyor from the Village of People Who Fish in the Lake
   Had a child with the journeyor
   Who had once been a slave,
   But lost the child.
   They traveled to the Town where Everyone Spoke a Different
      Language.
   They crossed the Sea of No Waves.
   They stayed on the Island of the Better Than Golden Time.

ANNOUNCEMENT: Returning Home
   (*The curtain is quickly closed and opened.*)
SONG.
   And so the Journeyor who left the Village
   Of People Who Fish in the Lake
   And journeyed to find the king,

29

And journeyed to find the beast,
And was a stranger in many places
Left the Island of the Better Than Golden Time
And journeyed back again to the Village
Of People Who Fish in the Lake.

She stood in the middle of ruins:
Her mother's bones,
The ashes of her father's books.
There was no one.
Everyone had gone.

(*The Journeyor, alone, has returned to the Village. The couple who whispered to each other in the first scene are like a memory on the platform in front of the side box. Another villager is a memory too, sitting on the two-step unit, his head between his knees. A ghost appears in the c. box [which now has no rear burlap curtain, it is possible to see through to the back of the theater]. An actor plays the concertina but without making music, just a breathing sound.*)

JOURNEYOR. Are you alive?

(*There is a single drum beat.*)

Are you dead?

(*Drumbeat.*)

Am I imagining you?

(*Drumbeat.*)

GHOST. I am between worlds, waiting.
For over a thousand years our village made nets.
For over a thousand years we continued making nets.
But there was less and less water in the lake.
Little by little we starved.

Your grandmother went away.

(*A musician in the playing area faces the ghost and accompanies some of what she says on the violin.*)

You went away.
Your brothers died here.
Your parents died here.
Of all the people in the village I was the last one to die.
After I had buried the final two in the floor of the lake
I covered myself with the net and lay down.

(*The violin plays again.*)

30

I cannot tell at exactly what moment I became dead.
I watched while birds came and pecked at my body.
I felt small animals dig up through the lake bottom and eat at my
  flesh.
The sun dried what meat was left on my bones and that meat was
  chewed by wolves.
I saw this and I felt it, but from a distance.
And so I knew I was dead.

Now the boundaries of my memory are broken.
I remember all that I ever heard or felt or dreamt.
I remember each being that ever touched me.
The world I lived in is more familiar to me now than when I lived
  in it.
Where I am now is unfamiliar to me again.
Bury my bones
And I will continue my journey.
  (*The actress playing the Ghost closes the curtains of the box.
The actors walk around the c. of the stage in a very slow circle,
accompanied by the breathing sounds of the concertina and a few
notes on the violin. Finally the Journeyor is left walking alone in a
circle. When in the singing area the other actors form two rows.
The front row is seated. The back row is standing and swings back
and forth like mourners.*)
SONG.
  And then she buried the bones of the ghost
  In the floor of the lake.
  She could no longer
  Come back to this place.
  And what would be the use
  Of the Golden Time in her village?
  What would be the use?
  And then, and then, and then, and then
  And then she ran into the Forest With No Roads
  And then she traveled for several days.
  And then she was wet and hungry
  And then she came to the House of the Hermit.
  (*There is a different musical sound before and after the next an-
nouncements than there were accompanying the previous ones.*)

(*The Journeyor reaches the Hermit's house which is the box* R.,
*as it was before. She squats on the platform and bangs hard and
rhythmically with two pieces of wood, expressing her desperation.
The Hermit answers her only after a time.*)

HERMIT. Go away.

(*She continues to knock.*)

Go away.

(*As she knocks we see behind her the Hermit's hands surreptitiously pulling the curtain back to have a look at her. She does not
see this. The curtain goes back.*)

You will not be able to look at me.

Leave me alone.

My face is hideous.

(*The Journeyor is still knocking.*)

Wait.

(*She stops. He finally comes out, wearing his mask. He hands
the Journeyor a green watch cap like his own. She puts it on.
The Hermit moves very slowly. He sits on the piece of sawed-off log. The Hermit hands the Journeyor a root to eat. He eats one
too.*)

SONG.

Then the journeyor and the hermit stayed together.

They played music.

They cut wood.

They gathered food.

They watched the sun set.

(*The Hermit hands the Journeyor a kazoo and she plays it while
he plays a wooden pipe. They are accompanied by a musician on
the tympani. They watch the sun set. Then they lie down to sleep
on the platform, sleeping "spoons" facing the audience, his gnarled
hand lying on her shoulder.*)

Then the journeyor and the hermit stayed together.

They played music.

They cut wood.

They gathered food.

They watched the sun set.

They slept.

They played music.

They cut wood.
They gathered food.
They watched the sun set.
They slept
Together.

(*The Hermit sits on the sawed-off tree trunk. The Journeyor sits at his feet, her arm around his leg. He pulls off his mask. His face is set in a wooden way under it.*)

HERMIT. There was the year a hunter came and burned down my hut and I had to build it again.

There was the year when the woods were filled with owls.

There were many years I didn't count.

And then you came.

(*There is quick journeying music. The Journeyor remains seated on the platform alone.*)

SONG.
And then, and then, and then, and then
And then, and then, and then, and then . . .
Then the journeyor from the Village of People Who Fish in the Lake
And the journeyor who was a hermit
Lived together in the Forest With No Roads
For a long time.

Then the journeyor from the Village of People Who Fish in the Lake
Traveled from the forest
To the City Where There Were Only A Few People Left.
And there she found her grandmother.

ANNOUNCEMENT: Wandering on.
The Story of the Grandmother Who
Was Four Hundred and Six Years Old.

(*In the c. of the stage the Journeyor steps down two steps into her grandmother's house. The Grandmother wears a dark kerchief. She sits on a stool [facing the audience]. In front of her is a cooking pot. The Journeyor kisses her grandmother and holds her. The Grandmother caresses the Journeyor's head in her lap and looks straight ahead. The Journeyor speaks as if she had just run a long way, she is out of breath.*)

33

JOURNEYOR. I stood in the middle of ruins:
My mother's bones.
The ashes of my father's books.
Everyone was gone.
   (*The Grandmother does not have an "old" voice but her movements are very slight and slow.*)
GRANDMOTHER. I'm listening.
I'll make tea.
I'll boil water for tea.
JOURNEYOR. In the king's courtyard
People were sick,
Some had no limbs,
Some were blind,
They didn't look at me.
They clutched at my clothes.
They spoke different languages.
The king sent me to kill the beast.
He said it had claws.
He gave me a task.
   (*The Grandmother puts the pot down.*)
GRANDMOTHER. I will help you.
I will tell you what to do.
I am four hundred and six years old.
I have lived in many places.
I had a child.
My mother died.
I left our village.
I had a lover who was a builder.
The war came.
We traveled from my country to his country.
A night I wrote letters by candle.
I became ill.
My lover died.
I sold myself to a man who bought lives.
We rode to the frontier.
We were caught between one country and another.
I was put in prison.
I loved a woman who was in prison with me.
I lived in a large field that had been a city.
I washed.
I cooked.

I carried water.
I made fire.
I picked up bits of wood, to burn, to sell.
I lived with survivors.
My bones became brittle.
I rode in a cart.
I lived by the side of an ocean.
I had a child.
When the child grew up he became a soldier.
I loved a man who came from the mountains.
We lived on the mountain with goats.
We heard the sounds of war.
I fed many men and many women.
I had a child.
When the child grew up she ran away.
I loved a woman who was dying.
I came to live in the city.
I am four hundred and six years old.
I had thirty children.
I have seen twenty wars.
Tell me what happened.
I'll help you.
I will tell you what to do.
JOURNEYOR. I saw a person hanging.
I cut her down.
But she hung herself anyway.
   (The Journeyor is still breathless.)
I went to the market.
I saw the beast.
I tried to kill it but I only cut down the tree.
   (While pouring water from the pot the Grandmother "freezes.")
I stopped looking for the beast.
The village was gone.
I wandered.
I lived with a hermit.
I became a hermit.
I wandered on.
I came here
   (The Journeyor notices the Grandmother has stopped.)
Are you holding your breath?
Grandmother?

It's me.
Can you hear?
Are you there?
She's stopped.

(*The Grandmother is "frozen" facing the audience. The Journeyor faces the audience too, standing on a step.*)
SONG.

The one who was my grandmother is ended.
The one who was four hundred and six years old
Is ended.
My mother's mother is ended.
The one who left her own country
Is ended.
The one who traveled is ended,
Who had thirty children is ended
The one who saw twenty wars
Is ended.
The one who was ill,
The one who was hungry,
Who saw the beast,
The one who cooked and swept her house,
The one who made tea
Is ended.
The one who said she would tell me what to do,
The one who was four hundred and six years old
Is ended.
The one who was my grandmother
Is ended.

ANNOUNCEMENT: The Last Scene of the Play
(*The last scene is a dance. The Journeyor, still standing on the
step, moves in rhythm and repeats the words "And then." Three
people, two of them recognizably from the Courtyard, move in
rhythm slowly under a net. The images presented by the actors
overlap, all parts of the stage are used. The Hermit joins the Journeyor and they dance to the back playing their musical instruments. The Person Who Could Never Stop Crying walks in circles
around and around the stage. The characters are not always played
by the actors who played them originally. In the c. box the Ghost
appears, and one of the Vibrating People from the Marketplace.
Below the c. box the actress who played the Journeyor rhythmi-*)

36

cally portrays the Fugitive. The actress who played the Hanging
Person rushes to the singing area and mouths singing. Then with
another actress she sits on the ground as the Journeyor and the
Hanging Person did when they went to sleep. In the c. box now
with the curtain closed two pairs of hands and feet dance as in the
Marketplace. The Speaking Person from the Courtyard comes in
holding her hair up, twirling. She moves faster and faster. Two actors in unison do the scrubbing on the steps motion from the Courtyard, while another actor does the Afflicted Person whose head was
in and out of her knees. The Hanging Person climbs the scaffolding
as if to listen to the Dreamer. The Masturbating Person from the
Courtyard. The head gestures of the Person Hiding Under the
Stone. The Blind Beggar walks through rapidly and in rhythm.
Many images are presented simultaneously. The Hustler from the
Marketplace. As one of the Puppeteers enters with a puppet in his
mouth the tempo picks up. He dances in fast circles, holding up the
puppets in his hands. The Couple from the Village. Two actors
take up the "And then" movement of the Journeyor: a repeated
one foot forward motion, but without going anywhere. In the back
the Journeyor stands on the sawed-off tree trunk and portrays the
Treebeast, moving slowly but in rhythm. The Angry Couple from
the Marketplace. Someone is dancing with the bucket from the
Courtyard over his head. The Speaking Person from the Courtyard
moves her broom rhythmically back and forth. Three do a dance
from the Marketplace. The Grandmother in the back with her pot.
An actress wearing part of the net holds the rag doll of the Hanging Person at her waist and marches about the stage in rhythm.
One actor uses the concertina. The words "And then" are repeated
by everyone. The Hermit says once "The woods were filled with
owls." The words "In the stone, in the child", "Is ended, is ended."
"Stitch", "You run and you run and you run and you run" are
picked up by different actors. All are facing the audience, moving
back and forth toward the front of the stage repeating now familiar
gestures and words. The music is more and more insistent. In
rhythm the actors leave and sit. Three women are left: the woman
with the rag doll at her waist and wearing the net, the Journeyor
portraying the Grandmother with her pot, and in the middle of
them the Hanging Person. Each dances in her fashion. The other
two leave the Hanging Person alone on the stage. She still has the
jump rope around her neck. She dances a fierce dance of exuber-
ance and joy. Then she dances off.)

37

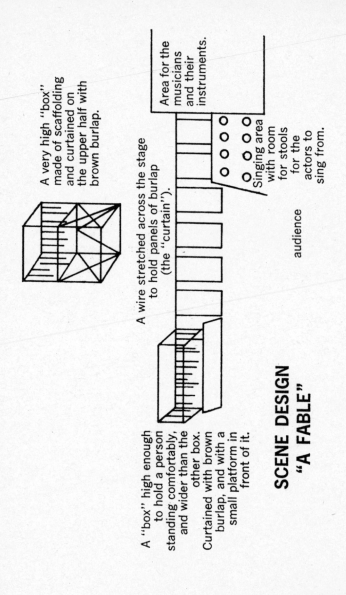

A very high "box" made of scaffolding and curtained on the upper half with brown burlap.

A wire stretched across the stage to hold panels of burlap (the "curtain").

A "box" high enough to hold a person standing comfortably, and wider than the other box. Curtained with brown burlap, and with a small platform in front of it.

Area for the musicians and their instruments.

Singing area with room for stools for the actors to sing from.

audience

SCENE DESIGN
"A FABLE"

38

PROP LIST BY SCENE

Village:
The net (preferably should not look brand new)
A shuttle to repair the net
Some string to repair the net
A soft cloth pack (dark blue) for the journeyor

Courtyard:
A wide old push-broom that makes noise when pushed
An old wooden scrub-brush
A wooden bucket
A small old wood washboard

Stone:
A periscope (a facsimile thereof)

Puppeteers:
Two simple handpuppets

Marketplace (This will vary with different productions.):
Various pieces of cloth
Various musical instruments, including concertina
A pair of black ribbons with large shiny discs sewn on (for Charm
    Seller)
A wooden stick (for Blind Beggar) preferably unpainted

Hanging Person:
A jumprope (child's)
A water bottle covered with cloth

Hermit's House:
A couple of sticks for journeyor to bang on
A kazoo or other small musical instrument for journeyor
A wooden pipe for hermit
A couple of turnips or other roots to eat

Grandmother:
A simple old cooking pot, small

NECESSARY PERSONAL COSTUME PIECES

Two green watchcaps (for use in Marketplace and Hermit scene)
A simple dark kerchief, easily put on, for Grandmother
A small ragdoll for Hanging person
Simple undyed cloth mask for Hermit with two eyeholes only

FURNITURE

Two wide three-tiered step units that can easily be moved around by the actors (not used after the Person Under the Stone scene)

A small two-step unit

A piece of sawed off tree trunk

A small wood stool (for Grandmother)

Other modest wood stools (for singing area, etc.) of various heights

A burlap-covered board

THE HUNTER
AND THE BIRD

THE HUNTER AND THE BIRD was first played as part of a Monday night Open Theatre presentation at the Sheridan Square Playhouse in New York City in 1964. The actors were Sharon Gans and Ron Faber; the director was Joseph Chaikin. Later productions include Danish TV, Theatre Company of Boston workshop production, and the Chicago City Players.

CHARACTERS

THE HUNTER

THE BIRD

THE HUNTER AND THE BIRD

The Hunter enters with his gun on his shoulder.

HUNTER. The hunter. I am the hunter, I hunt.

BIRD. (*To the audience, unseen by the Hunter.*) To hunt, to hunt, what he does is to hunt. (*She walks behind the Hunter, stepping in his footsteps, imitating his large walk—he doesn't see her.*)

HUNTER. I love what I do, and what I do is to hunt.

BIRD. He's a big man, this hunter. I— (*She comes to the audience and bows.*) am the bird.

HUNTER. I am the hunter.

BIRD. He is the hunter. He hunts.

HUNTER. I hunt.

BIRD. But I am the bird. (*She is the bird for a bit, fluttering and flittering around the Hunter. He doesn't see her.*)

HUNTER. I hunt for birds.

BIRD. Oh, lovely hunter. I am a bird. See my wings, oh see me fly. Oh, I am flying. I am a merely bird. I am flying. I fly. Flying. Fly.

HUNTER. Ha, ha, I see her. I see a bird. (*He puts his gun in shooting position. He revolves and wheels around.*) Bang. Bang. Oh, bang. Bang. Bang.

BIRD. Hee hee! He shoots! He shoots! Oh warpled day, he shoots!

HUNTER. I shoot, oh bang—bang, bang. Boom. Boom. Bang. A hit.

BIRD. I'm hit. I fall. Falling. Fall. Down. Ground. Here.

HUNTER. (*Facing the Bird for the first time in a "real" way.*) So.

BIRD. Hello.

HUNTER. I've got you. Right where I want you too.

BIRD. Who are you?

HUNTER. I'm a hunter who's got you.

BIRD. You have a lovely gun.

5

HUNTER. Yup.

BIRD. I have no name that I can remember.

HUNTER. I don't care about your name.

BIRD. What a lovely day, it is, like every day a lovely day.

HUNTER. I don't care about that either.

BIRD. You are very big.

HUNTER. I'm pretty strong for my age, yup.

BIRD. Strong. I almost love you, Strong.

HUNTER. I couldn't care less about that. Get on your knees.

BIRD. My knees? Birds don't have knees.

HUNTER. Don't give me fancy stuff. Do you know what I want from you?

BIRD. What do you want from me? I'll give it. I'll give it. Just tell me and I'll give it. What do you want from me?

HUNTER. I want you to tell me.

BIRD. Tell you what?

HUNTER. Tell me the secret.

BIRD. What secret?

HUNTER. I don't want to play games.

BIRD. I love games.

HUNTER. I'm going to wrench it out of you.

BIRD. Wrench what? What what, Strong?

HUNTER. I'm going to pull out your toenails.

BIRD. You're going to pull out my toenails? Oh no. What for? Oh no. Don't do that. No no no. It'll hurt.

HUNTER. It'll hurt. You bet it'll hurt.

BIRD. *I* bet it'll hurt. *You* bet it won't hurt.

HUNTER. I bet it *will* hurt.

BIRD. Well, if we agree then what's the point? Game's off.

HUNTER. Huh?

BIRD. I don't want to play the hurt game.

HUNTER. Are you going to tell me or am I going to have to pull out your toenails?

BIRD. Oh, I'll tell you. I'll tell you anything at all. Just ask.

HUNTER. Okay, bird, you sing.

BIRD. (*Sings.*)

> My love is a wanderer
> Wandering over land and sea
> And I am a wonderer,
> Wondering does love love me.

6

(She laughs and laughs.)

> Oh troo lee ar dee, loo dee loo dee
> Up by Charlemont way.

HUNTER. Okay for the toenails. *(He wrenches off her toenails.)*

BIRD. Oh! Red! Red! Horrible red. Jagged stripes of purple and red! Oh that's what the color of pain is. Deep horrible red! Love me!

HUNTER. Now will you speak?

BIRD. I'll speak. I'll speak. The color of my true love's hair is red. I'll tell you anything you want to know. I'll give you everything.

HUNTER. Teach me how to fly.

BIRD. How to fly? Like this. *(She flies.)*

HUNTER. Just tell me how. I've got a little notebook right here and I'll just write it down in a systematic manner and that'll be that. Right?

BIRD. Right.

HUNTER. Well?

BIRD. Well what?

HUNTER. Tell me how to fly. I've got people waiting for me. I mean to get this information.

BIRD. Information is a word I never heard before this moment. Information is a beautiful word. IN FOE MA SHUN. So nice. Like a lullaby. Information. Information me the sugar, please. Would you take my little information? Where is the information, please, I'm cold. Can you eat information?

HUNTER. How do you fly?

BIRD. Like this. *(She starts again. He stops her.)*

HUNTER. No, not that again. I have no time for demonstrations. I simply want you to tell me in clear concise terms.

BIRD. Oh yes, well. You take one wing and you lift it slowly and just as you've got it almost to the top you take the other wing and slowly you lift it up to meet the first one which is already on its way down and they pass each other only they don't speak, like strangers on the road, and then the same thing only faster, and you're flying.

HUNTER. Suppose you don't have wings?

BIRD. No wings? Well. Maybe little wings?

HUNTER. No wings. How do you fly?

BIRD. Oh look it's raining.

7

HUNTER. That's another question. How do you rain?

BIRD. That's easy.

HUNTER. How then?

BIRD. Pour. Just pour and then do it a little less and then you're raining. I want my toenails back.

HUNTER. (*Packing up to go.*) I want them for my records.

BIRD. May I have the gun?

HUNTER. You're putting me on.

BIRD. Just for a minute?

HUNTER. For a minute? Sure, Bird. Here. (*Bird takes gun. Bird shoots Hunter.*)

BIRD. Hoorah, hoorah. Oh frabjous day. He's dead. Kaloo Kalay and the bird she flew away. (*Bird flies away.*)

CURTAIN

PROPERTY PLOT

Personal:

Gun, which should not look real (The Hunter)

ALMOST LIKE BEING

ALMOST LIKE BEING was first staged in 1964–65 in New York City by Joseph Chaikin with actors from the Open Theatre; it played at the Vandam Theatre as part of the Playwrights Unit there, and at the Sheridan Square Playhouse on successive Monday nights. It was published in the Tulane Drama Review, and seen on television on channel 13 in New York City and over the Canadian Television network.

CHARACTERS

Narrator

Doris

Rock

Bud

Knockefeller

Billy

This play is to be done as if it were a movie being shot by several cameras. When the individual actors are not, for a moment or two, on camera, their expression is deadpan and bored. They are "turned on" for their "bits." Often Doris will make a facial expression especially for the camera, or she will address it instead of another actor. The actors will always know exactly where the camera is at a given moment—sometimes a closeup, sometimes a two-shot, panning, etc. This technical device should serve as a comment on the action.

ALMOST LIKE BEING

NARRATOR. (*Over the mike, under the movie music.*) A busy recording studio of one of the greatest companies in one of America's greatest cities. They are setting up for Miss Doris D. And yes, entering the room now in a small golf cart, is Miss D. herself. (*In comes Doris, wearing simple but gorgeous rehearsal clothes. She greets the few hundred people on the sound stage. Somehow when she greets one in particular, a certain Rock, there is a certain something deep in his voice, and a bell rings.*)

ROCK. Hello, Miss D. Hi there. (*The bell rings.*)

DORIS. Why hello to you.

ROCK. Miss D., I've set your levels at 440. Is that all right?

DORIS. Perfect.

NARRATOR. (*Over the mike.*) Miss D., we're ready when you are.

ROCK. 440?

DORIS. Ah, marvelous.

ROCK. 440, Bud.

BUD. Right, check, Rock. Here we go, Miss D. All America is waiting.

DORIS. I don't care how many times this happens. I'm always on my tippytoes, always. But I can only do my best, and with God's help, I'll get by.

NARRATOR. (*Over the mike.*) This is it, Doris. Sing. (*Doris sings a few lines from "When I Fall in Love, etc." Somehow her eyes seem constantly to stray to the control booth where a certain Rock is diddling the dials. Narrator, over the mike.*) Doris, Honey, perfect, just perfect.

DORIS. Oh, thank you, Mike. You really liked it? You're not just saying that? Thank you, Hal. It's so hard to tell yourself. Bill, thank you. I feel much better hearing that. Thank you, Stanley. Thanks Harris. Little Will. Oh Frank that's sweet of you to say. Chad when you're on the boom I simply trust, that's all, I trust. Thanks Charlie, you're the important one, keeping the studio in apple-pie order. Give my love to Oleander and the kids. Irving,

5

I love you. Dear Chad. Godfrey, Harris, Bob, Dover, Port, Jeremy, Jonathan, Rhia, Gwenn, Fred, Joe, Tania dear, Lee, Jack, Jeff, Dwight, Paul, Sam, Kevin, Hiram, Sid, Earl, Robert, Alan, Arthur, Ray, Leonard, Asa, Jay, George, Llewellyn, Alexander, Larry, Caesar, Franz, Adolf, Hans, Wolfgang, Rolf, Henri, Pierre, Jean-Claude, Jean-Pierre, Jean-Paul, Charles, Ivan, Alyosha, Dmitri, Nicola, Boris.

BUD. (*Whispering to Rock.*) She never forgets a name.

ROCK. She is just the greatest.

DORIS. Paolo, Juan, Pietro, Giovanni, Nebuchadnezzar.

ROCK. I can't tell you what it does to me when she opens her mouth.

DORIS. And Bud, thanks a heap.

BUD. Thanks to you, Miss D.

DORIS. And thank you, Mr. uh uh uh uh . . .

ROCK. Uh uh . . .

DORIS. Uh uh . . . (*A bell rings.*)

ROCK. Rock. The name is Rock.

DORIS. Thank you, Mr. Rock.

ROCK. Just Rock is fine.

DORIS. Just Rock then.

NARRATOR. (*Over the mike.*) Lock it up, boys. (*Doris and Rock snap out of it.*)

DORIS. Goodbye, all. I wish I could kiss every one of you here. (*She blows a little kiss. She leaves.*)

BUD. Hey, Man. Did she ever give you a tumble.

ROCK. (*Still in a daze.*) Yeah, yeah. What?

BUD. Some guys have all the luck. Now take me, the other day I was on the elevator and—

ROCK. Hey! Elevator!! Hold it!!! (*He rushes to the elevator and reaches it just in time to hold the door open and squeeze in scrunched right up nose-to-nose with . . .*) Oh. Hi.

DORIS. Hello, Just Rock.

ROCK. Almost didn't make it.

DORIS. (*Putting on her sexy face.*) Mmmmmmmmmmmmmm.

ROCK. Kind of crowded in here.

DORIS. (*Still with sexy face.*) Mmmmmmmmmmmmmm.

ROCK. Am I crowding you?

DORIS. (*Putting on her proper face.*) No. I'm fine.

ROCK. I could maybe move my arm a little down this way.

6

DORIS. (*Her very proper face.*) Don't bother, Mr. Rock.

ROCK. Just Rock.

DORIS. (*Her relenting face.*) Okay, Just Rock.

ROCK. Gee, I've never been so glad the studios are sixty-five floors up.

DORIS. (*Her coy face.*) Oh, and why's that, Rock?

ROCK. Well, it gives me a chance to talk to a star.

DORIS. (*Her simple face.*) Oh, Rock, I'm not a star. Sarah Bernhardt, now *that's* a star. I'm really nothing but a television, radio, theatre, and motion picture actress doing her best. And really underneath, well, I'm just *the* girl from Dubuque.

ROCK. Dubuque?

DORIS. Dubuque. *The* girl from Dubuque.

ROCK. Isn't that strange how some things, well . . . my mother was raised in Dubuque.

DORIS. Oh. Well then do you know, maybe you know a little diner out there in the West called Mango Pete's?

ROCK. Mango Pete's? Do I know Mango Pete's?

DORIS. Oh my heavens you know Mango Pete's? Why I had chocolate—

ROCK. Banana vanilla pistachio triple frappes with cherries.

DORIS. And the sign over the counter said:

ROCK and DORIS. (*Together.*) "We don't serve anyone over twelve." (*They laugh together joyously.*)

DORIS. (*Unnoticed.*) Where am I? I feel sick . . . what a small world.

ROCK. It certainly is.

DORIS. (*Unnoticed.*) If I don't get some air I'm going to suffocate.

ROCK. (*Unnoticed.*) I get nervous on elevators. What if the cable broke.

DORIS. Small and funny and nice.

ROCK. Yeah nice. (*Unnoticed.*) What if it broke right now?

DORIS. (*Unnoticed.*) I think I'm going to puke.

DORIS and ROCK. (*Together.*) Small and funny and nice.

ROCK. (*Unnoticed.*) I can feel it breaking. Crashing downward. This is it. (*He closes his eyes.*)

DORIS. (*Unnoticed.*) I'm suffocating here. No more air. I can't breathe at all. (*There is a while of terror until they reach the bottom, during which she is suffocating and he is sure he is plunging*

7

toward death. As the elevator door opens, sprightly.) Well, here we are.

ROCK. Yes. Well, well . . . could I ask you to lunch, Miss D.?

DORIS. (*Obviously in a quandary.*) Well, I'd love to. I'd really love it. But the fact is, well, someone is waiting for me.

ROCK. (*Devastated, but taking it like a man.*) You mean you have *Someone?*

DORIS. Well, not exactly *Someone*, but someone is waiting for me for lunch. As a matter of fact, it happens to be a certain Mr. Knockefeller.

ROCK. Well. I guess that's the breaks for the little guys like me.

DORIS. Oh, no, I didn't mean—

ROCK. Don't mention it. I'll be all right. There's only one place for the little guy.

DORIS. (*As a heavenly choir humming "This is the Army, Mr. Brown" swells under this tragic scene.*) One place?

ROCK. The khaki. It's the khaki for Rock. This is the army, Mr. Rock.

DORIS. Oh no. But let me explain.

ROCK. (*Trying his goddarndest to be brave.*) Don't bother yourself, Miss D.

DORIS. But I'm only going to see him for lunch.

ROCK. I'll be all right.

DORIS. Only lunch.

ROCK. So long little pater. It's been keen. (*He sniffles only once and stalks off, scuffing his foot against a stone. She starts to run after him.*)

DORIS. Rock! (*She stops herself, putting her hand over her mouth.*) Darn. (*She stops in a very businesslike fashion and fixes her hair. Life must go on. But at the door of the restaurant she has one more uncontrolled outburst.*) Darn, darn, darn. (*Cocktail movie music. She enters the restaurant. Knockefeller, an older man with graying temples, is seated alone at the corner of the table, a solitary martini in front of him. Doris, very businesslike, pulling off her gloves.*) I need a drink. Order me a lemonade. (*She pulls out a hand-mirror and powders her nose. During the whole cocktail scene both she and Knockefeller smile and wave at various friends they see around the room.*)

KNOCKEFELLER. Do you realize . . . ?

DORIS. Order me a lemonade please.

8

KNOCKEFELLER. Waiter, a lemonade for the lady.

DORIS. Must you order so arrogantly?

KNOCKEFELLER. Arrogantly?

DORIS. Yes arrogantly. I said arrogantly.

KNOCKEFELLER. Do you know I've been waiting here two hours?

DORIS. I can't help that.

KNOCKEFELLER. Do you know what happens to the world bank while I'm here two hours?

DORIS. Oh I don't care a fig about the world bank.

KNOCKEFELLER. Now Doris, that's not very considerate.

DORIS. In fact I don't care a fig about . . .

KNOCKEFELLER. Go on. I can take it.

DORIS. Oh Barry, I'm sorry. You know I don't mean to be sharp. That's not the real me. What with my career and this whirl-a-gig life you're leading me it's too much. I'm under the heaviest pressure.

KNOCKEFELLER. It's okay, Dorrie. Drink your lemonade.

DORIS. I'm sick of lemonade.

KNOCKEFELLER. How about some champagne?

DORIS. At lunchtime? At lunchtime? Oh you and your big ways. I can't go on like this, Barry. I'm sorry. I'm simply not built that way I guess. You have to have had a coming-out cotillion I guess to get used to champagne at noon. I'm just the girl from Dubuque. I was raised on triple malted frappes at Mango Pete's.

KNOCKEFELLER. At Mango Pete's?

DORIS. Yes, darn it, at Mango Pete's. Oh you and your yachts. I can't give up my career for some old yachts.

KNOCKEFELLER. I never asked you to give up your career.

DORIS. You're from another world, Barry. We're from different worlds. An artist, a *real* artist is an *artist*. I can't give up my career. You mustn't ask me any more.

KNOCKEFELLER. But who's asking?

DORIS. Well, then. I've made my decision. Duty calls and I have much work to do before I sleep.

KNOCKEFELLER. Is this it?

DORIS. I'm sorry, Governor, but goodbye.

KNOCKEFELLER. Little Dorrie.

DORIS. (*Sincerely.*) I'm so sorry for you. (*She rushes out of the restaurant.*)

9

KNOCKEFELLER. Oh well, back to tired old whores.

DORIS. (*Alone for a moment outside the restaurant.*) I'm all alone. (*Cut to backstage that night at the nightclub. Doris' Negro maid Billy, dressed as a nun, is dressing Doris in her Madonna costume.*) I can't go on tonight. I just can't go on. Not tonight.

BILLY. Miss D., Honey-lamb, is something the matter?

DORIS. Everything, Billy, everything. Sometimes life is like an angel-food cake that will never rise again.

BILLY. Is there anything I can do, Miss D.?

DORIS. Nothing, Honey, nothing. Just be your own sweet self. I don't know what I'd do without you.

BIILLY. Oh Miss D. Honey you know I'll stand by even if you were starving and old and ugly and all your arms and legs were gone and you were blind and deaf and had warts all over your face and couldn't sing no more. I'd stand by. You know I would.

DORIS. I know it, Billy. You're my one friend in the world.

BILLY. Oh, Miss D. You can't know what it means to me to hear you say that.

DORIS. Is my veil on straight?

BILLY. Just as straight as straight as straight as straight can be. You look just fine, Miss D. Just fine. I've never seen you look so fine.

DORIS. My crucifix.

BILLY. They're calling for you, Miss D. There must be thousands and thousands and thousands of people waiting for you, Honey, your public what you owe everything to. They love you, Miss D. Just think of that. How much they love you.

DORIS. Yes, yes I owe it to them. But thousands of pebbles don't make up for one Rock.

BILLY. Oh, Miss D. (*The applause having risen to a deafening pitch, out goes Miss D. to the footlights. They cheer and whistle. She manages a wee smile. The crowd is delirious. She holds her hand up for silence.*)

DORIS. My dear friends. My dear, dear friends. (*She holds up her hands in a plea for silence. The applause dies down just enough for her to be able to repeat her song. Doris sings same song as in studio, but with much more feeling now that she's been through so much.*) "When I fall in love . . ." (*After the first line, the public, in gratitude for having been given its favorite song, bursts again into wild applause, and Doris once again is*

10

obliged to hold up her hand to keep them quiet.) "It will be completely. Or I'll never fall in love. In this restless world we live in, life is ended before it's begun. And too many moonlight kisses dry in the warmth of the sun." *(Suddenly, behind her, who should appear, wounded and in uniform, but Rock. The Nun-Maid is overjoyed for Miss D.'s sake but Rock signals her to keep quiet until the song is over.)* "When I fall in love it will be completely or . . . I'll . . . never . . ." *(She sees Rock! She is so overcome she can hardly finish the song. She smiles at the audience, trying to keep up the show.)* ". . . fall . . . in . . . I— . . . love." *(At the end of the song, she rushes into Rock's arms. The audience, witness to all this, claps deliriously for both Doris and her boyfriend. She tries to pull him up to take a bow with her but he is shy. She finally succeeds. The audience goes wild. Doris and Rock join hands in what is to be the finale.)*

DORIS and ROCK. *(With gusto.)*

> An instant ago my feet were solid on the ground
> A moment ago I was sad but safe and sound . . .
> But suddenly you're near
> And now you're really here
> And oh, *this* is the hour
> And *this* is the place
> And all at once the stars . . .
> Are grinning at every soul alive!

(On the words "every soul alive" Doris takes the Nun-Maid by the hand and she joins them in the singing. Then Knockefeller appears on the sidelines. Doris beckons to him. He takes the Nun-Maid by the hand, and instantly you know these two were really meant for each other all along. Knockefeller also reaches over and shakes Rock's hand. Then all holding hands they step in rhythm toward the audience singing the last lines of the song. The song should sound like every popular movie joyous ending.)

DORIS, ROCK, BILLY and KNOCKEFELLER.

> And me, well I'm grinning too,
> And me, well I'm feeling too
> Like its nearly,
> Like its almost,
> Like its very nearly almost,
> Like its almost like being—

(On the last words—"it's almost like being"— they freeze in silence, wide smiles on their faces, and the lights black out.)

PROPERTY PLOT

On Stage:

Table and 2 chairs
Martini glass

Off Stage:

Small golf cart

Personal:

Purse, with mirror and compact (Doris)

Selected List of Grove Press Drama and Theater Paperbacks

B108 BRECHT, BERTOLT / Mother Courage and Her Children / $1.95

B333 BRECHT, BERTOLT / The Threepenny Opera / $1.95

E441 COHN, RUBY (Ed.) / Casebook on Waiting for Godot / $3.95

GT422 CLURMAN, HAROLD (Ed.) / Seven Plays of the Modern Theater / $6.95 (Waiting For Godot by Samuel Beckett, The Quare Fellow by Brendan Behan, A Taste of Honey by Shelagh Delaney, The Connection by Jack Gelber, The Balcony by Jean Genet, Rhinoceros by Eugene Ionesco, and The Birthday Party by Harold Pinter)

E159 DELANEY, SHELAGH / A Taste of Honey / $2.95 (See also Seven Plays of the Modern Theater, Harold Clurman, ed. GT422/ $6.95)

E380 DURRENMATT, FRIEDRICH / The Physicists / $2.95

E612 DURRENMATT, FRIEDRICH / Play Strindberg / $1.95

E344 DURRENMATT, FRIEDRICH / The Visit / $2.95

B215 DYER, CHARLES / Staircase / $1.95

B132 GARSON, BARBARA / MacBird! / $1.95

E223 GELBER, JACK / The Connection / $3.95 [See also Seven Plays of the Modern Theater, Harold Clurman, ed. GT 422 / $6.95]

E130 GENET, JEAN / The Balcony / $2.95 [See also Seven Plays of the Modern Theater, Harold Clurman, ed. GT422 / $6.95]

E208 GENET, JEAN / The Blacks: A Clown Show / $2.95

E577 GENET, JEAN / The Maids and Deathwatch: Two Plays / $2.95

E374 GENET, JEAN / The Screens / $1.95

E615 HARRISON, PAUL CARTER (Ed.) / The Kuntu Drama / $4.95 (Kabnis by Jean Toomer, A Season in the Congo by Aime Cesaire, The Owl Answers and A Beast Story by Adrienne Kennedy, Great Goodness of Life by Imamu Amiri Baraka (LeRoi Jones), Devil Mas' by Lennox Brown, The Sty of the Blind Pig by Phillip Hayes Dean, Mars by Clay Goss, The Great MacDaddy by Paul Carter Harrison)

E457 HERBERT, JOHN / Fortune and Men's Eyes / $3.95

B154 HOCHHUTH, ROLF / The Deputy / $3.95

E427 HOFMANN, GERT / The Burgomaster / $1.50

E456 IONESCO, EUGENE / Exit the King / $2.95

E101 IONESCO, EUGENE / Four Plays (The Bald Soprano, The Lesson, The Chairs,* Jack, or The Submission) / $2.95 *[See also Eleven Short Plays of the Modern Theater, Samuel Moon, ed. B107 / $2.95]

E646 IONESCO, EUGENE / A Hell of a Mess / $3.95

E506 IONESCO, EUGENE / Hunger and Thirst and Other Plays / $3.95

E189   IONESCO, EUGENE / The Killer and Other Plays (Improvisation, or The Shepherd's Chameleon, Maid to Marry) / $3.95

E613   IONESCO, EUGENE / Killing Game / $2.95

E259   IONESCO, EUGENE / Rhinoceros* and Other Plays (The Leader, The Future is in Eggs, or It Takes All Sorts to Make a World) / $2.45 *[See also Seven Plays of the Modern Theater, Harold Clurman, ed. GT422 / $6.95]

E485   IONESCO, EUGENE / A Stroll in the Air and Frenzy for Two or More: Two Plays / $2.45

E119   IONESCO, EUGENE / Three Plays (Amédée, The New Tenant, Victims of Duty) / $3.95

E387   IONESCO, EUGENE / Notes and Counter Notes / $3.95

E496   JARRY, ALFRED / The Ubu Plays / $3.95

E633   LAHR, JOHN (Ed.) / Grove Press Modern Drama / $5.95 (The Caucasian Chalk Circle by Bertolt Brecht, The Toilet by Imamu Amiri Baraka (LeRoi Jones), The White House Murder Case by Jules Feiffer, The Blacks by Jean Genet, Rhinoceros by Eugene Ionesco, Tango by Slawomir Mrozek)

B142   McCLURE, MICHAEL / The Beard / $1.25

B107   MOON, SAMUEL (Ed.) / One Act: Eleven Short Plays of the Modern Theater / $2.95 (Miss Julie by August Strindberg, Purgatory by William Butler Yeats, The Man With the Flower in His Mouth by Luigi Pirandello, Pullman Car Hiawatha by Thornton Wilder, Hello Out There by William Saroyan, 27 Wagons Full of Cotton by Tennessee Williams, Bedtime Story by Sean O'Casey, Cecile by Jean Anouilh, This Music Crept by Me Upon the Waters by Archibald MacLeish, A Memory of Two Mondays by Arthur Miller, The Chairs by Eugene Ionesco)

E410   MROZEK, SLAWOMIR / Six Plays: The Police, Out at Sea, Enchanted Night, The Party, Charlie, The Martyrdom of Peter Ohey / $4.95

E433   MROZEK, SLAWOMIR / Tango / $3.95

E568   MROZEK, SLAWOMIR / Vatzlav / $1.95

E462   NICHOLS, PETER / Joe Egg / $2.95

E650   NICHOLS, PETER / The National Health / $3.95

E393   ORTON, JOE / Entertaining Mr. Sloane / $2.95

E470   ORTON, JOE / Loot / $2.95

E567   ORTON, JOE / Complete Plays / $4.95

B354   PINTER, HAROLD / Old Times / $1.95

E315   PINTER, HAROLD / The Birthday Party* and The Room: Two Plays / $2.95 *[See also Seven Plays of the Modern Theater, Harold Clurman, ed. GT422 / $6.95]

Critical Studies

Grove Press, Inc., 196 West Houston Street, New York, N.Y. 10014